PUNCH YOUR INNER HIPPIE

Also by Frank J. Fleming

Obama: The Greatest President in the History of Everything

How to Fix Everything in America Forever:
The Plan to Keep America Awesome

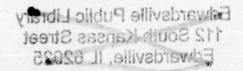

Punch

Your Inner

Hippie

Cut Your Hair, Get a Job,
and Make America Awesome Again

FRANK J. FLEMING

ILLUSTRATIONS BY HUNTER J. SEXTON

BROADSIDE BOOKS
An Imprint of HarperCollinsPublishers

HarperCollins books may be purchased for educational, business, or sales promotional use. For information, please e-mail the Special Markets Department at SPsales@harpercollins.com.

FIRST EDITION

Library of Congress Cataloging-in-Publication Data has been applied for.

ISBN: 978-0-06-230243-4

14 15 16 17 18   ov/rrd   10 9 8 7 6 5 4 3 2 1

To Buttercup and Frankie, two good reminders that I can't be a whiny hippie.

Acknowledgments

First, I'd like to thank my lovely and talented wife, who edited the first draft of the book and gave me great feedback and who is always supportive and puts up with my crazed mood swings when I'm in Pretentious Writer Mode. Thanks to my mom and dad, who taught me good values and a strong work ethic, some of which stuck. Thanks to Adam Bellow and the entire HarperCollins team for giving me the opportunity to see what my writing is like when it's longer than a blog post or a tweet. Thanks to my beta-readers Harvey, Basil, and Charlie. Thanks to Glenn Reynolds, Jonah Goldberg, Rick Moran, John Siniff, Mark Cunningham, Bill Whittle, John Hawkins, Rachel Lucas, and all the others who encouraged me along the way in my political humor career. And a special thanks to all the readers of my blog, IMAO, for all the support throughout the years. Though we haven't yet nuked the moon, we've struck fear in its heart.

I also want to thank the Founding Fathers, George Washington, Benjamin Franklin, Ronald Reagan, and Mr. T, who made this great country and all the opportunity it's provided me. And finally, thanks to God, without Whom the earth would be without form, and void, and there would be little to write about.

Contents

PUNCH YOUR INNER HIPPIE

1

What's Holding You Back

It's dangerous to go alone! Take this.

—old man giving a small child a lethal weapon

In the long, long ago, the frontiersman pushed the boundaries of this country. He set off by himself into the unknown, heading west. No government was there to help him, and he had no guarantee of food or shelter—and certainly not safety. He was truly on his own in the wilderness. Think of what went through his mind when, while exploring some woods, he heard a low growl and turned to see a mountain lion standing next to him, ready to pounce. He couldn't call the police or animal control for help, and there was no hospital to treat his wounds. What do you think the frontiersman did? Scream? Run? Fall down and cry?

Of course not. Instead, he simply punched that stupid mountain lion right in the face. Sure, he had a rifle, but ammo was scarce out there, and he needed to save it for real threats, like angry native people who had a more legitimate claim to the land. The frontiersman was an American—a real American—and there was no way some putty-tat would be a threat to him. And after that mountain lion ran off crying with a broken nose, the frontiersman chopped down a bunch of trees, fastened them together to build a crude Walmart, and then sold goods to other frontiersmen and became rich.

The average American in days of yore.

Those were just things Americans did back then: punch wildlife and build businesses. These people were true innovators—the kind of people who saw a raccoon and thought "hat." And they didn't have any of the advantages we have today, like computers or the Internet or cell phones—a text message back then had to be sent by horse—yet nothing could stop them. And when they encountered a problem, they dealt with it in the most direct way possible: a punch to the face.

Now, let me ask you a question: Are you like the frontiersman?

No, you're not. Right now, you're just sitting there reading a book like some doof. But that's okay; you don't know how to be that type of American yet. You're more like the mountain lion after its chance encounter with a frontiersman: confused. A little scared. Somewhat dizzy. But don't worry; this book will help you even better than a wake-up punch to the face.

Don't you want to meet your full potential as an American? Instead of being someone who cowers from adversity, do you want to be someone who will put a grizzly bear in a headlock and throw it through a plate glass window? Someone who could have a dollar one day and a multinational corporation the next? Someone who will see a rocket, see a car, and say, "I should make a rocket car!"?

Of course you do; that's the American everyone wants to be. And meeting your full potential as an American means you'll easily be able to:

- Create a business
- Master your finances
- Attract the opposite sex
- Build the perfect plate of nachos
- Get lots of Twitter followers
- Strangle two communists at once
- Collect all the Triforce pieces in Legend of Zelda
- Make cool YouTube videos of explosions
- Get other countries to fear you

It may sound too good to be true, but Americans like that used to be the norm, and you can be like that as well.

So why do some people succeed and meet their full potential as Americans, and others, given the same opportunities and advantages, just suck? Why do some Americans create corporations, invent advanced technologies, and have Internet memes written about how awesome they are while other people in the same country are just blobs sitting on couches, staring at screens, and munching prepackaged foodstuffs?

There's a simple answer, but to understand it, we have to look at why great civilizations fall. Is the United States itself in decline now? Some would say so. Look at what America was in the past: We chased out the British, became the most powerful nation in the world, defeated the Nazis, invented nuclear weapons, and landed on the moon. And what have we done lately? Well, our phones get new features every year.

Look at what Americans were able to achieve in the past when they had relatively little, then think of what they could do with our technology and advantages. By the end of the year, there would be giant robots stomping through the cities of our enemies, even the poorest citizens would have jetpacks and laser guns, and we'd have an ultralibertarian moon colony. So why aren't we doing that? What happened to our country that the highest an American ever aims to achieve now is beating the next level in Candy Crush?

I'll tell you why: hippies.

Whiny, smelly hippies who do nothing but sit around and whine, expecting everyone else to do the work for them. They are the bane of civilization.

And what can you do with hippies? Can you reason with them? Of course not, because whining isn't real speech and can't be refuted with reason. So what can you do with them? There's only one thing that can be done: Yell, "Shut up, hippie!" and punch them in the face like a common mountain lion. Now, have you ever heard about hippies living during the time of the frontiersman? Of course not; back then a hippie couldn't even fully open his mouth before getting punched. That's because it was an innate value instilled in Americans that hippies must be punched. It started when we punched those hippie British, with their silly tie-dyed coats* and love of higher taxes, and continued as we punched the Soviets because of all their collectivist ideals and the round fur hipster hats they wore. And it's why America became the greatest country in the world.

But at some point we lost that inborn knowledge that hippies must be punched. Americans became lazier and started to feel more entitled. Morality declined. Childhood obesity skyrocketed. Vampires started sparkling. The very soul of our country started to weaken. And today, everywhere you look, hippies are walking around, whining and spouting nonsense, and no one has the decency to punch them in the face to help them end that behavior.

So what does that mean? We need to all run around punching every hippie we see? Maybe. But will that achieve anything? Probably . . . but not enough to get our country back to where it was. Just go ahead and try it. Go out and punch a bunch of hippies.† I'll wait.

Did that make things better? Maybe a little bit. But are you now as capable as the frontiersman of yore, ready to go out and headbutt the day into submission?

---

* The British had only one color available for tie-dyeing: red.
† Punching a hippie may be considered assault in some areas. Consult with a lawyer before punching any hippies.

No. You're still a doof whose lack of achievement shames those who founded this great country. Imagine Thomas Jefferson with tears in his eyes; that's him reacting to what a disappointment you are.

So am I saying that punching hippies isn't enough to get this country going again? Of course not; unpunched hippies are central to all our problems. But we need to punch the right hippies. The problem now is so widespread that regular old hippie-punching will not fix things. Because the most dangerous hippie out there is no longer the one we see walking about the streets in tie-dyes and tinted glasses. Instead, it's the one inside us: the inner hippie. And to get ourselves and society back on the right path, that is who we need to punch hardest of all. Your shout of "Shut up, hippie!" and your fist both need to be directed inward.

And that's why I wrote this book. Back in the day, you could just punch a hippie and expect him to automatically know why you did that, but society has declined so much that people don't even understand why you're punching them for hippie behavior anymore. You need to give them an explanation along with this punch, and that's what you can consider this book: a punch to your face followed by a well-reasoned explanation of why that just happened.

Now, I know there are many self-help books out there, but they only ever tackle the symptoms of the problem. The difference with this one is that it focuses on the core of what causes you to fail: your inner hippie. And I'm going to show you step-by-step how to punch your inner hippie to finally get him to shut his stupid mouth. I am this country's leading authority on American awesomeness. In addition, I have long studied the science of hippie-punching and its benefits to the individual and to society. And now I am going to apply that knowledge to help you punch your inner hippie—the one barrier holding you back from being all that you can be.

But punching your inner hippie is not an easy process. If you have a hippie-type whiny thought, can you just go to the mirror and punch yourself really hard in the stomach? You can try that—and it might help some*—but that is not going to defeat your inner hippie. To truly unlock all of your abilities, you need to thoroughly pummel the hippie inside you until he's a broken wreck who can barely move. And this is a long and arduous process. But I will walk you through it in this book, and when we're done, you will be an American whom all others will look upon with awe and fear—the way it should be.

So are you ready for this? If there's a little voice holding you back, saying, "I don't want to do this; this seems hard. Just wait on other people to fix things. This probably

---

* Punching yourself really hard in the stomach can cause health problems in some people. Consult with a doctor before punching yourself really hard in the stomach.

won't work anyway. And this guy seems kind of violent and crazy," that's just your inner hippie trying to hold you back once again. Your first punch against him will be to continue reading.

To help in your study, I got an unpaid intern to write up a summary of what you should learn in each chapter. Each chapter will also have some study questions to help you think on the concepts introduced, and then some answers to common questions.

CHAPTER 1:
WHAT'S HOLDING YOU BACK
SUMMARY

In this chapter, we learned:

- In the long, long ago, people were tougher, more innovative, and not as nice to wild-life.
- We've forgotten the simple American value of punching hippies.
- You can unlock your full potential as an American, but first you must punch your inner hippie somehow. I guess this book will go into that later.
- This is apparently the best self-help book ever.
- I'm going to summarize chapters in a chapter summary like this one.

In the next chapter, we'll look at the history of the hippie and how he's caused failure in every era throughout the world.

Study Questions

You have access to much better weaponry than the frontiersman, but if you turned right now and saw a mountain lion standing next to you, ready to pounce, would you be able to take it on? Why or why not? Do you even know how to tell a mountain lion from a large tabby cat?

When you hear the term *hippie*, does that have positive or negative connotations to you? If you said positive, what's wrong with you? I mean, come on.

Have you ever been punched for being a hippie? How did that make you feel? Did you shut up?

ANSWERS TO COMMON QUESTIONS

Q. Just to be clear, when you mention punching hippies, are you talking about physically striking hippies, or are you speaking metaphorically about "punching" hippies through rhetorical means or through your actions against narcissistic hippie ideals?
A. Um . . . yes.

Q. You say punching one's inner hippie will unlock one's true potential as an American, but will this also help people from other countries?

A. Well, I don't see how punching hippies could ever harm anyone, and I certainly recommend it for all, but I'm not quite sure what its effect would be on someone from another country. For instance, I don't know if it would unlock your potential as a "true Icelander"—I'm not even sure what exactly that would mean.

Q. What would happen if a hippie punched his inner hippie?

A. If one were all hippie and punched his inner hippie, there would be nothing left to take over, and that person would probably go comatose. Thus, being comatose, the person would still be as useless as his hippie self before the punching, but now less whiny, so this would still be a marked improvement, and I still recommend the application of a punch in that situation.

Q. Do you think the Founding Fathers really would cry if they saw us today?

A. Absolutely. I mean, first they'd have to get over the shock of the modern world and all of our technology, which would be like magic to them, and then I think the government would be really threatened by time travelers, so the Founding Fathers would have to flee their government pursuers. But once they found a proper hideout and figured out how to work a computer so they could see some YouTube videos, they'd be pretty upset with what has happened to us as a people.

Q. You don't think they'd find those cat videos funny?
A. Well, sure, some of them, but it wouldn't make up for the complete collapse of the hardworking, independent spirit in the modern American.

Q. And what about—
A. Know what? The book has just started. Why don't you hold your questions for a little bit.

2

Know Your Hippies

And knowing is half the battle.　　　　　**—General George S. Patton**

People often come to me and ask, "What is a hippie?"

To which I usually answer, "Why are you bothering me? Haven't you heard of Google?"

But then I checked to see what answers one might find on the Internet, and they are inadequate, completely missing the core of the problem with hippies. I tried to edit Wikipedia so it would have better information on hippies, but I was kicked out for "vandalism." So I went to Wikipedia headquarters to formally complain, but I was kicked out for "vandalism." Art can be speech; check your Constitution. Anyway, as usual, the Internet is completely useless (except for commerce, communication, education, and various other uses people are still discovering).

To defeat the hippies inside us, it's useful to know about hippies. "Know thy enemy," as I always say—though I think "thine" is more grammatically correct. But "thy" sounds better. Anyway, before we jump into punching our inner hippies, I want us to take some time to understand our enemy and know the history of the hippie and how he has tried to destroy civilization many times.

So what are hippies? Where do they come from? Why are they here? Why do they smell so bad? What do they have to do with tie-dyeing?

Merriam-Webster defines *hippie* as "a usually young person who rejects the mores of established society (as by dressing unconventionally or favoring communal living) and advocates a nonviolent ethic; broadly: a long-haired unconventionally dressed young person."* This is a stupid definition that completely misses the point. Here is a more accurate definition of a hippie:

hippie - *n - annoying, useless individual who does nothing but pester and drag down society. Often smelly, these individuals are the root of all failure in mankind. See* **punch**.

---

* Source: *Merriam-Webster's Dictionary*, somewhere between **hiccup** and **hippogriff**.

A HISTORY OF THE HIPPIE

It's not enough to simply be told what a hippie is; you need to understand how hippies have ruined everything throughout history. Now, it's a common misconception that hippies came about in the 1960s—that's just when the usual bulwark society constructs against hippies broke, and hippies felt free to roam about the land in their true form. Really, though, hippies have been plaguing society since the beginning of man. It's a little hard to tell who the hippies were in the long, long ago since everyone wore funny clothes back then, but with a little analysis of history, we can trace hippies back to their origins and begin to see how they first emerged.

The First Hippies

Who were the first hippies? The obvious answer is Adam and Eve. Now, I don't call them this because they pranced around naked all day like they were at Woodstock—it's because of their attitude. See, they were given paradise, but what did they decide? That they deserved more—namely the forbidden fruit. And that's a hippie attitude right there; no matter what a hippie has, he'll become ungrateful for it and think he deserves more. So when a snake came up and tempted Eve, she wasn't all like, "Shut up, snake!" and then punched him in the snake face. No, instead she ate the fruit and shared it with Adam, and then God had to come at them with some tough love—the only sort of love one should ever show hippies—and was all like, "That's it. You guys are out of here. You can't mooch off my paradise anymore and need to go find a job." And now no one can go to the Garden of Eden, because that's what hippies do: ruin things for everyone.

For the most part, though, hippies were actually very rare among early man. Think of the caveman, struggling every day just to feed himself and his family and survive. Where would a hippie fit in this scenario? Life back then would not support someone who did no work and just whined and complained.

*"Aren't you going to help in the hunt, chap? Cheerio."**

"No, man. I don't want to be a part of this mindless 'let's go kill a mammoth' culture."

"But if we don't hunt, we'll starve, mate. Can you at least sharpen some stones to use as spears, chop chop?"

"I'm a pacifist; I don't like weapons."

"If you're not going to hunt, could you do some gathering, eh? You really have to do one or the other."

---

* I don't know how cavemen talked, so I'm just guessing.

"No, man. You guys are just stuck in this old 'hunt and gather' mind-set. Instead, look at this buffalo I drew on the wall. That's art, man. That's important. You guys should be happy to do all the hunting and gathering to support my artist's lifestyle."

"Not sure I cotton to that one. And are you sure you should be eating those mushrooms, ese?"

"It helps my creativity!"

That nonsense would not fly back then. During those times, people had to spend all their effort on survival, so there would be no tolerance for someone who didn't help out and just annoyed everyone else. They would probably just hit that guy with blunt objects (as was the custom at the time). There is no way a hippie could survive in such times. If he didn't give up his hippie ways, he'd starve to death or freeze to death or be eaten by a giant sloth. So it was just not possible for there to be hippies in the long, long ago. The ironic thing is that for there to be conditions in which someone can lie around and complain all day, a society first has to advance enough that all the basic needs are well taken care of, that is to say, when there are no longer real problems, that's when the whiny hippie emerges.

Thus the first emergences of the hippie we see commonly in history are among royalty. In the first civilization, the common man slaved away long hours working crops or grinding flour or pounding out horseshoes or whatever stuff people did back in medieval times or earlier,[*] thus leaving him too busy trying to survive to engage in hippiedom. Only the royalty were well-off enough to complain about frivolous things and begin to become hippies.

"My mutton isn't cooked right, the bells in my jester's hat aren't ringing enough, and my gold crown is all itchy. Now get me some fresh kale, and make sure it's organic."

This is the fatal flaw of the monarchy: You can end up with hippies in charge of your country. And with all these hippies running everything, we got the Dark Ages, because hippies aren't going to do the hard work needed to advance society, like invent gunpowder or develop capitalism. But they will be so filthy that your society will get plague.

Wait, is my timeline right on all this? Let me check . . . eh, I'm close enough.

Still, as bad as things were, most people still had to work hard way back when and thus couldn't be hippies. But what happens when a civilization advances enough that hippies become prevalent throughout society?

---

[*]   My knowledge of that era mainly comes from the Game of Thrones books.

Hippies and the Collapse of the Roman Empire

The first society to advance far enough to become overrun with hippies was Rome. I mean, they had it nice for living thousands of years ago, with democracy, aqua ducks,* and guys yelling, "This is Sparta!"—actually, I guess that last one is the Greeks, but they're basically the same thing, I think. Anyway, they, like, conquered most of the known world—which was a lot, because they only didn't know about half of it—and things were pretty sweet. I mean, all roads led to Rome—like if you saw some road you didn't know and were like, "Where does this road go?" the answer would be "Rome" because that is where all roads went. You didn't even need signs to point to Rome—you'd just follow the road, and eventually you'd get there. And if you wanted to go somewhere else . . . I guess you'd have to just not take a road. But why would you want to go somewhere else? Rome was where things were happening.

So, the Romans got to thinking they were pretty special, and that is where the problem started. When people have things good, they start to think they're owed that lifestyle and that it will always be that way. And that's when the hippie-ism began to spread throughout Roman society. Soon

---

* I don't know what other types of ducks there are.

all Romans were hanging around in togas—and when you see a bunch of guys in togas, you know no one is up to any serious kind of work.

And to support the hippie lifestyle of hanging around in loose clothing and doing nothing, they kept adding more and more holidays. Eventually, half the calendar was filled up with holidays. And as you know, banks always have twice as many holidays as everyone else, so it got to the point that there was only one day a year that the banks in the Roman Empire were open. This became known as "Banking Day," and people began to celebrate it. And thus soon it became a holiday as well, and then banks were closed that day, and then no one could get to their money, ever.

So what happened to Rome and the Roman hippies? Well, one day, barbarians were at the gate. And, being hippies, instead of mounting a good defense, the Romans just said to the barbarians, "Come on, guys; just chill. Here, we'll give you some bread and throw you a circus." See, the Romans didn't really think anything could happen to them because they *deserved* their lax lifestyle, but they were wrong. The barbarians—led by Conan, I think—sacked Rome and burned everything. And now there is no more Rome.

Well, actually, I just checked the map, and there is still a Rome . . . but it's not nearly as good anymore. I mean, barely any roads you find will actually go to it. And while it is the capital of Italy, it's not like it's anything special anymore. I mean, when big things happen on the world stage, everyone isn't going, "Hey, we'd better find out what Italy thinks about all this." No, instead they just look at Italy and say, "Hey, you look like a boot. How cute." No one would call Italy bootlike and cute if Rome were still a superpower.

But that's what happens when you let hippies run rampant. Still, hippies can do much worse things than destroy a country. Last century, we got to see what happens when hippies gain power and nuclear weapons.

Hippies and the Rise of the Soviet Union

So early last century, the Soviets rose up and started conspiring together in Russia.

"Man, we should have like a socialist revolution."

"Yeah, and stuff should be given to people based on need instead of how hard you work and stuff."

"Totally. And there should be a dictatorship of the proletariat."

"Um . . . I dunno what that means, but if you're talking about the government giving me stuff, I'm totally for it."

Now, what would usually happen in a situation like this? The hippies would express their ideas to the general public, and the general public would say, "Shut up, you stupid hippie," and punch the hippies in the face. And that would be the end of it.

But no one punched these hippies, and during a time of political unrest, they actually took charge. And then what happened?

Oppression. Starvation. Murder. Mustaches. Lots of Photoshop for some reason.

People have this idea that hippies are peaceful, but scratch a hippie and you'll find a fascist—which is why you don't scratch them; you punch them. The only reason hippies often seem harmless is that they usually have no power to do anything. But if they get that power like they did in the Soviet Union, they will hunt down and murder anyone who questions their hippie ways. That's right: In Soviet Russia, hippies punch YOU!

So let that be a lesson: If you don't punch the hippies, and you let them rule, it's basically the worst thing imaginable. Especially since eventually the Soviet Union got nukes and pointed them at us. And then they were all like, "We're going to defeat evil capitalist America and make the whole world Communist and then . . . oh, wait a second. I have to go stand in line for bread."

Hippies and the United States

On our last stop in this historical exploration of the hippie, let's look at hippies and the United States. As I said before, it's incorrect to believe that hippies first arose in America in the 1960s. That's simply when society declined enough that hippies could come out into the open and not even bother trying to hide their uselessness. But there is evidence of hippies throughout American history.

For instance, think of the root cause of slavery. Basically, there were people who wanted to force others to do all the work. That's a pretty hippie move when you think about it. And when slavery ended, the hippies who had infiltrated society just tried to find other ways to get everyone else to do the work—mainly through government and taxation. Taxes would take money away from people who worked, and then the government would give the money to those who didn't. It's the hippies' love of mooching written into law. This really expanded in 1913, when the Sixteenth Amendment was ratified, allowing the government to collect income taxes. Who would vote to give the government more taxation powers? That's like voting for larger mosquitoes.

Of course, we all know hippies became loud and proud of their complete uselessness in the sixties. Soon the United

States was infested with drugged-out, lazy, annoying hippies. It was starting to look like the end of America, especially in the seventies with President Jimmy Carter, who watched the economy collapse and society crumble and otherwise did nothing because he was too busy being bullied by rabbits. But after him came Ronald Reagan, who implemented a strict "hippies must be punched" policy. Like when the Speaker of the House was all like, "We have to be careful about being too mean to the Soviets. They're not bad people," Reagan walked right up to him and uttered his famous quip, "Shut up, you stupid hippie!" and punched him in the face. America got the message, and there was a huge decrease in hippie-ism throughout the nation. Soon, the country prospered, and then we developed Star Wars lasers so we could destroy the Soviet Union. To this day, you can go to the Reagan Library and see Mikhail Gorbachev's head mounted on a pike.

But after the Soviet Union's collapse, America started to get lazy again in the nineties. People assumed prosperity would just go on forever, and then we got things like the dot-com bubble—you can see the hippies' fingerprints all over that one. Everyone was all like, "All these websites are super-worth lots of money even though none of them turn a profit!" It was basically just the hippies' idea of getting money for nothing, but done in this high-tech way that fooled lots of other people into going along with it.

And then came our new enemies: the terrorists. And you'd think the threat they pose would help America focus and get away from hippie ideas, but it wasn't long before there were hippies everywhere, saying things like:

> *"You can't be mean to the terrorists; we have to understand them."*

> *"This violence is just a result of our own foreign policy."*

> *"Don't waterboard terrorists; such cruelty will only create more of them."*

Pouring water on terrorists doesn't create more of them! They're not gremlins!

Rarr! Stupid hippies!

And aren't terrorists in a way just hippies with bombs? I'm not sure on that, because I've never bothered to understand terrorists and just want them shot.

And now where are we as a nation? We elected the first black president to try to eliminate racism, but it didn't work; I still hate the Irish. And hippies still run rampant in our country with nary a punch thrown. We have a bloated government, a complete collapse of our economy, and a bunch of generally whiny people who frankly aren't pulling their weight compared to the Americans of old. It looks pretty bad, and we could be seeing the end of our great nation. And the end won't be in some awesome nuclear battle with the Soviets like we once thought it would be. Instead we'll die with a whimper, surrounded by useless, whining hippies.

Unless *you* prevent it. Yes, you reading this book right now. Only you can prevent the destruction of America by hippies. And forest fires. Actually, don't worry about the forest fires—that more concerns stupid squirrels and owls or something. Just worry about the hippies.

TYPES OF HIPPIES

Now that you understand that hippies have been a plague on civilization throughout history, it's time to learn about the common types of hippies we usually encounter. While all hippies are annoying and awful, they come in many different forms. Here are the ones I know of:

Traditional: The traditional hippie is the stereotypical one with long hair and a tie-dyed shirt who is constantly stoned and is very smelly. They're actually kind of rare these days, since during the hippie-punching days of the eighties, most hippies learned to at least try to hide their hippieness. If you see one like this, it's kind of a freebie. But before you punch away, check the date, as it's actually pretty likely that it's just someone in a Halloween costume. And it's a pretty good one, too, because what makes more sense to see going door-to-door demanding free stuff from people: a ghost, a goblin, or a hippie?

Environmentalist: This is a common hippie these days who is constantly going on about how we need to save the earth. From what? Asteroids? No, they want us to save it from, like, plastic bags and car emissions and spray deodorant—really asinine stuff. Come on. The earth has been around somewhere between 4.5 billion and 6,000 years—considering who you ask—and it's like 30 percent iron, but now all these hippies called "environmentalists" act like we're hurting it. These are just people who can't deal with real problems like terrorism, nuclear rogue states, and the existence of foreigners in general—things that take hard work to combat—and instead want to focus on made-up problems that can be solved with dinky stuff like recycling your aluminum cans. The earth and the life on top of it have survived meteors and volcanoes and the cancellation of *Firefly*, so it doesn't care if I regularly spend hours doing donuts with a Humvee for no reason. Don't let these hippies waste your time—any time spent recycling is time you could have spent designing a giant robot with Gatling guns for arms. Now that's how you protect a planet.

Celebrity: There are lots of ways to get famous these days. You can make viral YouTube videos of yourself freaking out over a rainbow. You can go on a high-speed car chase; cops love those, because they get bored. Maybe you could write a book; I'm not sure if that works anymore. Of course, one of the most traditional ways to become famous is to pretend to be someone with useful skills in a TV show or a movie. Another way is to sing and dance really well—like a more sophisticated version of the organ grinder monkeys from days of yore. There's nothing inherently wrong with any of this, but the problem occurs when these people think that because others know who they are, that means we are all interested in their ideas and opinions. If they actually had any useful knowledge, though, they'd be saving an office building from well-funded European terrorists in real life instead of pretending to do that on shows or singing for our amusement as we perform useful labor. Anyway, the celebrity is a very privileged yet often inherently useless person and a type of hippie who is these days unfortunately looked upon with reverence by too many people instead of with the sort of disdain one might have for any other sort of loudmouthed incompetent. Just because you've heard of someone doesn't mean you should have.

Politician: You might say, "Hey, politicians aren't hippies. They look all sophisticated in suits and stuff." Well, that's just a hippie trick to get you to trust them. Politicians are indeed hippies if you just think about it: They have no useful skills (many of them are lawyers), they produce nothing of use to society, they are extremely irritating, and they like to act like they know everything and tell people what to do. It's pretty odd that out of all the different groups of people we could put in charge of things, we keep choosing politicians when they're the absolute worst for it. Usually, if a hippie came up to you and said, "I want to make laws and boss you around," you would just punch him, but you can't punch politicians, or you will get tackled by Secret Service agents. What kind of scam is that?

Vegan: Vegetables taste awful. This is a scientific fact. Some people may claim to like certain types of vegetables. They are lying. They are all awful. And there is no way to cook them in which they don't have that horrible vegetable taste. There is, in fact, only one way to make vegetables taste good: feed them to an animal, which then through natural processes turns that into tasty meat. But some hippies, called vegans, being mindlessly countercultural, have decided to shun all the tasty foods that come from animals and only eat horrible vegetables. These types of hippies are easy to identify because they will not shut up about it ever. And they think this shunning of everything good and tasty makes them healthy and gives them superpowers or something. That's hippie nonsense. The fact is, not consuming meat makes you crazy. It's called "mad not-eating-cow disease."

Hipster: A very odd sort of hippie in that they are quite prevalent these days yet intensely hated by everyone to the point that no one will actually admit to being one. Anyway, they like irony and vintage shirts. Also, I want to point out that I intensely hated hipsters before it was cool.

Journalist: So the idea of a journalist is someone who just repeats to you what's going on—he's like an advanced form of parrot. But in practice he's more like a hippie, trying to influence your opinions. This is a horrible idea, because hippies are very bad at thinking. And these hippies become journalists not to just give you simple facts, but to change the world by getting the "important" facts out. Of course, their minds are too twisted by hippie-ism to know what's actually important, so mainly they just ignore bad stuff about people they like and then harp on bad stuff about people they don't like—and they constantly go on about it for a week straight. Hey, I honestly thought that man was a yeti when I hit him with my truck, and I don't know why they would inject "racism" into that; yeti is not a race. Anyway, you end up dumber when you let yourself be "informed" by these nitwits. Go around the journalists and get your news from the Twitters and blogs and such. Yeah, a lot of that is nonsense, but if you stick to traditional journalists, you only get nonsense from one side, whereas if you seek out the news yourself, you'll get a more balanced nonsense.

Baby: Babies are basically hippies. All they do is cry and complain until someone else handles whatever they think is wrong. Also, they expect other people to give them everything while contributing nothing. The big difference between babies and other hippies is that they should grow out of this. Also, unlike with other hippies, you shouldn't shout at babies and punch them.* Another difference is that babies sometimes smell nice.

Lawyer: This is another one where you're probably like, "Those ones aren't hippies. They're successful, well-groomed people who wear suits." Well, yes, it seems that way, but think about it like this: Do lawyers actually produce anything for society? No, they just bludgeon with stupid laws the people trying to do useful things. What do you mean I can't open a fireworks factory on my own property? And what's a zoning law? Sounds like some sci-fi nonsense. Anyway, while lawyers are hippies, it's not a good idea to punch lawyers, as they'll sue you for everything you've got if you do. In fact, they might sue you for slander just for calling them hippies . . . or libel if you write it in a book. Know what? Forget I said anything about this one.

Canadian: I'm not actually sure these are hippies—they just weird me out. I mean, they're a lot like Americans—but

---

* Source: Most child care books.

not quite. Something is just off about them. I'm not sure what they are. And it freaks me out. I'm not saying punch everyone who ends a sentence with "eh," I'm just saying keep an eye on these people.

SUMMARY FOR CHAPTER 2: KNOW YOUR HIPPIES

In this chapter, we learned:

- The author is basically just making up the definition of a hippie.
- Hippies apparently have been around since the very beginning, using primitive bongs made from chiseled stone, I guess.
- Rome must have had lots of traffic problems with all those roads going to it.
- If hippies are in charge, the world will be threatened by nuclear annihilation, and you'll have to stand in line for bread (unless you're gluten-free).
- Apparently slavery can be blamed on hippies. And I'm guessing the Nazis were hippies, too. I don't know how he skipped over Nazis.
- There are many types of hippies. If you don't like someone, he's probably a hippie. See first bullet point.

Now that you know all about hippies, in the next chapter we'll talk about the most dangerous hippie of all: the one inside you.

Study Questions

If you had a time machine and could go back in time and punch the hippies who somehow went unpunched and caused the collapse of society, would you? Or is this like a going-back-in-time-and-killing-Hitler thing where the change in history could cause even more problems?

Was Hitler a hippie? Maybe a hipster? Do you think that mustache was ironic?

How many of the different types of hippies listed in this chapter have you punched? What were the results for each one?

ANSWERS TO COMMON QUESTIONS

Q. Isn't it simplistic to reduce the history of civilization to how much hippies have influenced society?
A. No.

Q. Isn't your answer to the last question simplistic?
A. No.

Q. Where did you get all your information on world history?

A. Internet.

Q. Could you be more specific? Like, what websites did you consult?

A. Google.

Q. Can you give more than one-word answers to questions?

A. Yes . . . I can.

Q. Anyway, it just seems like your take on history here is a little sketchy with the facts.

A. I understand what you're saying, but that's not a question, so I'm just going to ignore it.

Q. So are you saying society would not have problems if there were no hippies?

A. Like a society where everyone gets along, and there is no poverty or war, and we all dance and sing songs together? No, of course not; that sounds awful and boring. We'll just be able to upgrade to better problems, like maybe fighting off an alien invasion or some awesome conflict like that.

Q. Are you saying if we became a hippieless society, we'd get attacked by advanced, warlike aliens?

A. I'm saying that when we are a society no longer dragged down by hippies, we would be able to take on such an attack. And it would be awesome. I mean, think of how interesting the History Channel would be years from now, when it's all about the details of us fighting off the Zerfnor.

Q. The Zerfnor being the advanced, warlike aliens from your hypothetical scenario?

A. I thought that was obvious from the context.

Q. You seem to imply that all the people who use welfare are moochers, but aren't many of them in dire situations and in need of help?

A. If you were in a really bad situation and came to me and said, "Hey, Frank, some horrible things happened to me, and I need a few bucks to get by," I'd probably give you a few bucks if you seemed like an otherwise upstanding person. If you came to me and said, "Hey, Frank, some horrible things happened to me, and I want to raise your taxes and bloat the government until it's trillions of dollars in debt so it will take care of me," I would punch you in the face and call you a hippie.

Q. You listed a number of different types of hippies in this chapter, but could there be other types?
A. Absolutely. Hippies are creatures that will adapt to new forms of annoying uselessness based on the culture, and as some types of hippies disappear, new, more virulent strains of hippies can rise up. In that way, hippies are a bit like bacteria. One difference, though, is that there are useful bacteria—like those that aid in digestion—while there is no such thing as a useful hippie.

Q. If knowing is half the battle, what is the other half?
A. Probably firearms and bombs and stuff.

3

The Inner Hippie

You're making me whiny. You won't like me when I'm whiny.

—the Incredible Hippie

I knew this guy, Harold, who just could never get his life together. Anytime he started to learn some new skills for a new job or clean himself up, he'd eventually give up and go back to his bad habit of being lazy. He just putzed about his apartment with no ambition and no work ethic, achieving nothing. Well, he was pretty good at Call of Duty—often got some pretty big killstreaks there—but other than that, he was kind of useless. He finally came to me and said, "Desmond,* I just can't ever succeed. What am I doing wrong?"

---

* I don't give out my real name, so as to avoid identity theft.

And I told him, "You're not taking on the root of your failure."

He asked me, "What is the root of my failure?"

I answered, "Well, to find out, you'll have to buy my book when it comes out. I'm not giving this stuff out for free."

But he never did get my book, because he fell down an open manhole and died. That doesn't really have anything to do with my point, but you can't mention Harold and not mention the falling down a manhole, because everyone always says about him, "Oh yeah, that's the guy who fell down a manhole and died. It was like something from a cartoon."

But if Harold hadn't fallen down a manhole and had gotten my book, he'd be reading the answer to his question, which I am writing now. You see, there is something inside you that wants you to fail. Something in you wants you to go through life never achieving anything. Something that dwells within you wants all your dreams to shatter.

No, I'm not talking about a stomach virus or a tapeworm or demonic possession (but do get checked for all of those); I'm talking about your inner hippie.

Now, you may protest this. I just spent the last chapter telling you that the hippie is the reason for most of the ills of civilization and is the downfall of man, so I can see why you would be reluctant to admit that such a vile thing resides within you. But that hippie is there, and he is doing all he can to devise your failure.

You don't believe me? Why don't you go out right now and start a successful business.

So did you go out and create a business, or did you just sit there and say, "That sounds hard"? The latter, right? That's your inner hippie right there.

Yes, there is a hippie inside all of us, and he is the root of all our failure. Science has proven this.* And yes, it's scary to contemplate. Somewhere in you—out of range of any fist—is a shaggy, lazy, whiny hippie, smoking his weed and talking about how capitalism oppresses poor people. And he is why you are not the powerful American decimating all challenges that you should be.

So, you need to learn about your inner hippie and how to punch him so you can finally unlock your true potential. And if you don't defeat your inner hippie quickly, you could fall down a manhole and never succeed. Oh, see, I did work that into my point. I wish Harold could have seen that.

---

* Source: *Things Science Has Proven* by Scientists, page 324.

INNER HIPPIE TEST

Of course, how much everyone is affected by their inner hippies varies based on how much they allow these creatures to run rampant in their psyches. Here are some of the symptoms to look for that indicate problems of the inner hippie:

- Low motivation levels
- Scattered thinking
- Trouble connecting with people
- Offensive body odor
- Sore face

To see just how much your inner hippie controls you, I've devised this test. Go through the questions now and record your answer to each multiple-choice question.

1. Running a business sounds to you like . . .
   a. . . . a really hard proposition at which you're not sure how well you'd do.
   b. . . . a great idea and something at which you will easily succeed. Better start practicing your serious-looking pose for the cover of *Forbes*.
   c. . . . a bad idea, as it further promotes our unfair, capitalistic system.

2. Ninjas jump out of a tree and attack you. You . . .
   a. . . . run away.
   b. . . . fight them off with your kung fu skills.
   c. . . . try to understand the root cause of ninja hostility.
3. Every time you tell people your views . . .
   a. . . . people nod politely.
   b. . . . everyone basks in awe at your strong yet simple, coherent wisdom.
   c. . . . someone yells, "Shut up, hippie!" and punches you.
4. A man in sunglasses and a black trench coat offers you a choice of a blue pill that will leave your world the same and a red pill that will wake you up to reality. You . . .
   a. . . . take the blue pill.
   b. . . . take the red pill.
   c. . . . take one of the much stronger pills you brought yourself.
5. You have five apples. John has one hundred apples. John gets five more apples. How many apples does John now have?
   a. One hundred and five.
   b. It's kind of unseemly for me to be preoccupied with how many apples John has, but suffice it to say that he seems to have a lot. Perhaps I can

learn some apple-acquiring skills from him.

c. It's unfair that John already had many more apples than me and then got even more! The government should take some of his apples and give them to me!

6. While you're in the bathroom, armed terrorists take over the Christmas party you're attending. You . . .

a. . . . try to stay hidden and out of danger.

b. . . . sneak through the ventilation ducts and take the terrorists out, one by one.

c. . . . secretively start drafting new gun control legislation.

7. You sense an imbalance of wealth distribution in society. You . . .

a. . . . consider voting for socially conscious political candidates.

b. . . . are happy, because some people suck and should have less money.

c. . . . camp out in front of banks and make incoherent protests with no idea of exactly what you're trying to accomplish.

8. You're hungry. You . . .

a. . . . purchase some food.

b. . . . venture out into the forest, kill something, roast it over an open fire, and eat it.

c. . . . whine.

9. You come to a fork in the road. You need to know which path to take, and standing next to the paths are one person who always tells the truth and one person who always lies, but you don't know who is who. You . . .

   a. . . . ask one of them which path the other one would tell you to take and then take the opposite path.

   b. . . . say, "I don't have time for this nonsense!" and punch them both, then use the GPS on your phone to find the correct path.

   c. . . . stand there awhile and contemplate the relative nature of truth, wondering whether the one who always "tells the truth" is really any more truthful than the one who supposedly always lies.

10. You're tasked with taking an evil ring to a volcano—the only thing that can destroy it—within the enemy's territory. You . . .

    a. . . . set out by foot with a group of adventurers.

    b. . . . have the wizard summon a giant eagle to quickly fly you there and get this thing over with.

    c. . . . forget the quest and just sit around smoking pipe weed.

Now let's see how you did. For each A answer, add one point to your total; for each B, zero points; and for each C, two points.

If you scored 16–20 points: Not only is your inner hippie dominant, but you pretty much are a hippie. If I saw you right now, I would punch you. And you would deserve it.

If you scored 11–15 points: You're a borderline hippie. Your inner hippie controls a lot of your life, keeping you a constant failure. You could probably also use a shower.

If you scored 5–10 points: Functional adult. You're just the average person. And average makes baby George Washington cry.

If you scored 1–4 points: Successful adult. You've mainly conquered your inner hippie, but he still lurks in there somewhere, holding you back. It's time to finish him off.

If you scored 0 points: You're me, and you're taking this test as part of proofing your own book. Good job, Frank. It worked perfectly. You're awesome.

HIPPIE-ISM EQUALS FAILURE

People often ask me, "Can't a person both succeed and be a hippie? Do the hippie values of peace and love and being one with nature really run opposite success?"

My answer to that is to say nothing and just glare angrily

at the person until he sheepishly backs off and goes away. Because there is so much stupid in that question that there really is no good answer to it other than an angry glare.

Anyway, yes, hippie-ism equals failure. Success and being a hippie are two forces that oppose and attempt to destroy each other, much like if the town from *Footloose* that bans dancing took on the guy from the song "The Safety Dance" who has near-genocidal rage against people who don't dance. This isn't just opinion—it is science fact. Someone did an experiment where a number of hippies were locked in a room and had to solve a series of increasingly difficult puzzles to escape and survive. Eventually, all of those hippies were found dead.* When hippies have a task to complete, they will fail. So you need to beat down your inner hippie so you can follow the path to success.

Some may object, though, and say, "Well, aren't there successful hippies? What about those Ben & Jerry's guys? They're a couple of hippies who made a hugely popular brand of ice cream." That's actually the exception that proves the rule. Think about it: They eventually sold their company for millions of dollars to Unilever; does that sound like something hippies would do? Sure, they may have started out as hippies, but they became successful when they overcame being hippies and learned to run a profitable business and

---

* He actually may not have been a scientist and instead may have been a serial killer.

eventually had enough sense to sell it to a giant corporation for a huge profit. I'll bet that around the end, Ben and Jerry only kept up the hippie look for public appearances, but back in their giant mansions they relaxed in three-piece suits while smoking fine cigars they lit with hundred-dollar bills they stole from poor people, since the poor were only going to waste them.

Would you actually buy ice cream from a real hippie? Let's say you see some hairy, smelly guy by the side of the road with his product in a broken-down freezer, saying, "Want to buy my ice cream? It has big chunks in it!" Are you giving that guy your money? No, you're getting away from him as quickly as you can. And I'm sure that's what Ben and Jerry learned when they started out—that being hippies meant failure—and luckily the draw of capitalism and money led them away from their hippieness. Now they just use being hippies as a fashion statement on their ice cream cartons to attract gullible hipsters.

Origin of the Inner Hippie

So why does your inner hippie love failure? Well, it wants to convince you that you can't succeed. Because success takes hard work, and everyone knows there is nothing a hippie hates more than hard work. The only time a hippie comes close to breaking a sweat is when playing hacky sack. Thus your inner hippie tries to convince you that success is out of your control and that you should just loaf around all day, whining and being lazy and occasionally kicking around the hacky sack of failure.

But why do we have an inner hippie who tries to get us to fail? There are a number of guesses—exposure of early man to radiation, mummy curse, some sort of evolution-ary mishap like the one that got us the platypus—but my best guess is Satan. As part of the fall of man, Satan put a hippie inside each and every one of us to try to push us toward failure. I have no evidence of this—I tried consult-ing a number of demonology experts on the subject, but it always ended in a fistfight—but it fits all the data. If you're a demon who wants mankind to fail, then hippies are the perfect means to that end. Thus when you punch your inner hippie, you're not only improving yourself; you're also being pious.

Voices from Your Inner Hippie

So how do you know your inner hippie is at work trying to make you fail? Well, if you listen closely, you may notice voices in your head urging you to inaction and failure. Here's what those voices often say:

"You will fail."

"It's too hard; just give up."

"No one could actually do that."

"This isn't fair!"

"You'd look cool in tie-dye."

"Taking care of yourself is too difficult. Just vote for the guy with the D next to his name and let him do it."

These voices are exactly why you need to punch your inner hippie and tell him to shut up. It's hard to get motivated for success when some annoying, lazy part of you keeps urging you to fail.

There are other voices you might hear as well, voices that say things like "They're against you and must be punished" or "Kill them all!" That's most likely some other sort of psychological phenomenon than the inner hippie, and you should not do what the voices say and should instead seek psychological help—or do do what the voices say. I don't know; it's kind of out of the scope of this book.

THE MATRIX OF HIPPIE FAILURE

The best way to understand how the inner hippie causes failure is to look at the Matrix of Hippie Failure. It's not a cool matrix like the movie *The Matrix*, but is instead a depressing matrix (more like the sequels), as it reduces to the component parts what makes hippies such annoying, useless failures.

Laziness

Central to a hippie is laziness.

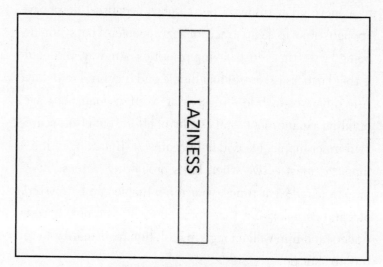

Matrix of Hippie Failure Figure 1

The hippie inside you does not want you to try to accomplish things, because accomplishing things takes work, and work is anathema to a hippie. Your inner hippie does not want to make the effort to achieve anything beyond mediocrity. He just wants everything to be handed to him, but the only thing he should be given is a fist. To his face. You should punch him in the face. See, I'm not lazy; I'll take time to explain things.

I once met a man who told me about all his troubles. He was failing at his sales job, was overdue on his mortgage, and just looked like a complete mess all the time. I looked him in the eye and told him, "Your problem is that you're lazy. Stop being lazy." And then he perhaps went on to achieve great things; I don't know, because I don't have enough time to keep track of lazy people. That's not my being lazy—that's just having priorities. Anyway, the point is that laziness is central to a hippie and is central to failure. Anything worthwhile—success at work, a good marriage, building a giant robot—takes a lot of effort, but effort scares your inner hippie. He will fight against it. In fact, your inner hippie is most active when he is promoting laziness. It's a bit of a paradox; at times, your inner hippie can be mysterious and complex, but that's okay, because you only have to understand him well enough to bash him really hard and get him to shut up.

Dependence

Branching off of the laziness is dependence.

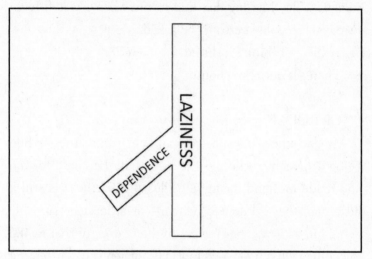

Matrix of Hippie Failure Figure 2

Your inner hippie feels that taking care of a human being—namely yourself—is a huge responsibility way beyond your abilities. Thus he will expect everyone else to take care of your worthless self. Anything he thinks you need—food, shelter, Wi-Fi—he expects to be the responsibility of someone else—basically those of us who actually do work—to provide. Of course, what is someone who is wholly dependent on others? A child. And do children achieve anything great? Maybe Doogie Howser, but not usually.

So this is one of the ways your inner hippie drags you

down, as you can't accomplish awesome things if you're not even the master of your own life. If your own basic needs are far beyond you, so much farther from your grasp is awesomeness. It's like my dad said to me when I was fifteen: "Are you a capable person?" he asked.

"Yeah . . . I think so," I said.

"Then get out of my house."

"What?"

"GET OUT!"

My dad knew that no one can achieve greatness while being a mooch, so he did the best thing he could for me and made me fend for myself. Plus, I think he was still a little mad that I'd dented his car—or at least presumably dented it, as it was hard to get to the bottom of that ravine to confirm what happened to it. Hey, when you're inventing a self-driving car, you're going to have a lot of vehicles flying off into ravines.

Anyway, what I'm saying is that your inner hippie is going to do all he can to keep you dependent on others and not responsible for yourself, and if you don't fight him, that's a big part of why you'll never have the momentum to succeed. Dependency removes all your capability and leaves you inert, like a car stuck in a ravine.

Faux Intellectualism

Also branching off of laziness is the way a hippie tries to sound smart: faux intellectualism.

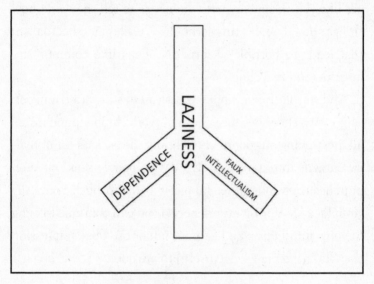

Matrix of Hippie Failure Figure 3

This is the lazy sort of intellectualism a hippie engages in. True wisdom comes from experience. That means that to really know things you have to go out and build things and climb things and punch things. Every scar you get gives you more knowledge than a hundred years of sitting around contemplating with a stupid hippie brain.

Still, the hippie, being lazy, wants to feel smart without doing all the work. He wants to just sit around and act like he has special wisdom to give the world despite the fact that the hippie is useless and stupid. Thus your inner hippie will compel you to do things like listen to some report on NPR about the plight of baby sloths in South America and then act like you're some expert who needs to tell the world how things should be. It's this sort of lazy, useless intellectualism that leads to horrible, destructive ideas like communism, fascism, and recycling.

And so your inner hippie wants you to stay away from getting experience, because the real world hippie-punches us all, destroying our poorly thought-out ideas as its fist of reality careens into our faces. Truly wise people seek out such punches, but your inner hippie will try to push you away from face-shattering experience so you can continue to cling to your dumb ideas and operate under the false impression that you have knowledge useful to anyone.

Whining

Surrounding all the parts of hippie failure is whining.

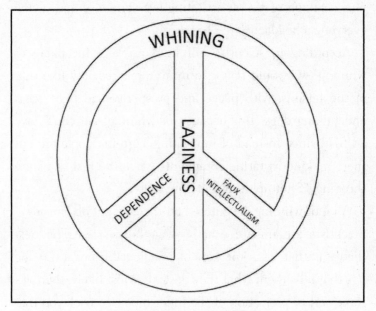

Matrix of Hippie Failure Figure 4

For the most part, hippies do not communicate; they just whine. Some people may think whining is communicating, but that is a common misconception. Whining is just failure made into an offensive sound, and it is one of the most prominent parts of the hippie.

There is little in this universe worse than whining. It's worse than famine and genocide and putting raisins in cookies instead of chocolate chips. Whining does nothing but destroy, because when someone is whining, he is not solving a problem. He's just annoying people. Thus whining compounds a problem, because now we have the problem plus a bunch of people irritating everyone else and giving everyone a headache.

According to scientists,* if humans were incapable of whining, we would now live in a utopian society like that of the Jetsons, with peace and prosperity and flying cars and talking dogs. But because of whining, we can't have all that, since instead of innovating, certain people are out there making irritating complaints while the rest of us are shouting, "Shut up! Shut up! Shut up!"

A lot of whining is centered on the concept of "fairness." Scientists are unsure exactly what fairness is. The best theory is that it's some sort of imaginary friend everyone has that tells them what they deserve. Most likely, then, it's some sort of projection of the inner hippie to trick you into a whining cycle of failure. The first indication that you may be about to whine is the thought popping into your head about something not being "fair." If you don't immediately slam your head against a table to jar that poor thinking, an epic whine could be coming, and I may not be nearby to assist you by punching you.

Of all the parts of the Matrix of Hippie Failure, whining

---

* To be honest, I don't really know the difference between a scientist and a random guy in a long white coat with lots of pockets acting knowledgeable about stuff.

definitely is the worst. If you had someone who was totally lazy, a complete dependent, and constantly spouted nonsense but didn't whine, he'd actually be tolerable. I mean, I wouldn't tolerate it, but the point is that even with all those awful characteristics, that person would still not be a hippie. Because whining is the *sine qua non*[*] of being a hippie and just about the worst thing ever.

Body Odor

Well, this one doesn't really fit into the Matrix of Hippie Failure, but I feel like I should also note that hippies smell bad. They just do.

---

[*] That's Latin.

SUMMARY OF CHAPTER 3: THE INNER HIPPIE

In this chapter, we learned:

- There is a hippie inside everyone other than Frank (possibly not his real name).
- The hippie is the root of all failure and constantly speaks to us, urging us to fail, because of Satan maybe.
- The inner hippie causes failure with the Matrix of Failure, which consists of whining, laziness, and I already forgot the others.
- You need to defeat your inner hippie before you fall down a manhole and die.

In the next chapter, we'll learn how you go about punching your inner hippie—kinda the crux of this whole book.

STUDY QUESTIONS

Think of times in your life when you've been a lazy, useless failure. Can you identify your inner hippie's influence in each of those times?

How does having a hippie inside you make you feel?

Did you answer that last question with an actual list of feelings? If you did, could you feel the influence of your inner hippie making you do something so asinine?

ANSWERS TO COMMON QUESTIONS

Q. Are there any scientific psychological studies that back up your thesis that a person's inner hippie is the root of all his failure?
A. Oh, come on. Psychology is not an actual science. Real science makes things like lasers and rocket ships. Psychology is just guesswork on people's moods and is completely unprovable.

Q. Actually, they do double-blind studies to—
A. Unprovable. And it's counterproductive. Psychologists always want you to whine about your father or something, but the more you whine, the more you fail. The heart of

your problem is always the hippie inside you, and if your therapist directs you toward anything other than delivering a severe beating to that whiny hippie, you will not get any better and are just wasting your time.

Q. But I had some extreme problems, and my therapist—
A. Waste of time. Don't want to hear it. Less talking, more punching. That's how you get better.

Q. You act like all dependency is bad, but isn't it good for society if people rely on each other?
A. You can combine forces with others to make greater things, like when peanut butter and chocolate combine to make a peanut butter cup. But they're not dependent on each other. Peanut butter is never like, "Well, chocolate isn't around; guess I can't do anything and will just crash on the couch all day." No, peanut butter is just going to go be part of a sandwich or try its best to make celery worth eating. You savvy?

Q. So I need to be peanut butter?
A. You wish you were peanut butter. Right now you're some weird Marmite spread or something. But if you follow the advice in this book, you can be peanut butter.

Q. **Aren't there things worth complaining about, and isn't it unfair to dismiss that as whining?**

A. "Unfair"? This sounds like a whine. Here's a tip: If you have a problem, instead of complaining about it, you just go solve it. Time spent whining is time not spent finding a solution, and nothing makes your inner hippie happy like your being useless.

Q. **Are there any drugs that can help suppress the inner hippie?**

A. Drugs? Now you sound like a hippie looking for the easy way out. The rest of this book will detail how to beat your inner hippie, and it's hard work.

Q. **How much hard work? This sounds like a lot of effort to—**

A. Uh-oh. I think your inner hippie is taking over. Quick! Punch yourself to suppress him!

Q. **That will suppress the inner hippie?**

A. At least temporarily. He's hitting you with laziness, and you're not going to finish this book unless we take quick measures now. Hit yourself.

Q. **I don't know if that—**

A. No time to think about it! Just do it!

Q. But—

A. DO IT!

Q. Ow! I think I might have hit myself too hard. I really feel like—

A. No, you're good. Let's move on.

4

Punching Your Inner Hippie

How do you beat up a whale? One punch at a time.

—ancient Chinese proverb

So I was working with someone who was really trying to tap his full potential, but his inner hippie kept pulling him down any time he tried to succeed. I think he was an accountant or something—all these people complaining about their problems just blend together. Anyway, let's call this man "Bob," as that's what I called him. I told him, "Bob, if you want to get anywhere in life, you first need to defeat your inner hippie."

"But I don't know how," he said. "It's not like I can just punch myself."

"Well, I can punch you," I said, "and I will, because I like to help. But I won't always be there. Instead, we need to find a way for you to really lay the smackdown on your inner hippie to silence its call to failure, and doing that will take some extreme measures. Come with me, Bob."

"My name's not Bob, by the way."

"I don't care. Come along."

I took Bob to the zoo after hours and headed toward the gorilla pit. "See that gorilla, Bob?"

"Wow," Bob said, "he's massive."

"Pretty intimidating, huh?"

"Yeah."

"Is that gorilla anything like a hippie?"

Bob thought for a moment. "Not really . . . except he probably doesn't bathe regularly."

"Correct. A gorilla is nothing like a hippie," I said, "and yet here is the thing: I want you to go punch him."

"What?"

And then I pushed Bob into the gorilla pit. The gorilla immediately became angry, since Bob was invading his territory. Bob started to panic and tried to find a way to escape. "No, Bob," I told him. "You need to stand your ground and just uppercut that stupid gorilla. I mean, just knock him out cold. Show him who's boss, okay?"

"Why?!" Bob screamed.

"Because it will be awesome, that's why. And I'm going to film it on my phone and put it on YouTube, and it will blow everyone's minds. Punching out a charging gorilla—that is so awesome. Just wrap your mind around that, Bob."

"I don't understand!" he pleaded.

"You will in time, Bob. You will in time."

"My name's not Bob!" he yelled, now in tears.

"Whatever, Bob."

You may have noticed that so far there has been a lot of emphasis in this book on punching, especially the punching of hippies. Scientists have long studied exactly how punching cures hippie-ism. The general consensus is that the blunt impact of the fist to the nerves of the face causes a surge of stimulation to the brain, often shocking it out of the poor, hippie-type thinking. Other scientists believe that hippies simply don't like to get punched, and thus punching them just gets them to shut up. Whatever the reason, a punched hippie is a much less annoying one and is much less of a drag on society.

But how do you punch your inner hippie?

The hippie inside you is the worst hippie of all, the one whose whining will drag you down the most, because he is always there and always trying to suppress you in his lazy, annoying ways. And one punch won't do it; that will shut up your inner hippie for a bit, but he'll soon be back in force, whining at you to give up and be mediocre. Instead, to defeat your inner hippie, you need to deliver him a constant and thorough beating so he never, ever has a chance to utter a peep.

But, of course, a physical bludgeoning isn't an option, because your inner hippie is a metaphysical concept. That's what is frustrating here. He's the worst hippie of all and constantly bothers you, but he's out of reach of your knuckles.

Being that he's a metaphysical concept, one way to deal with the hippie would be to find some place comfortable to relax where you can imagine this hippie inside and then visualize yourself hitting him over the head with a trash can. The problem with that is that the whole meditation thing seems kind of hippie-ish itself. Instead, there is a much better way to punch your inner hippie. And that is by being awesome.

Anytime you shake off the shackles of mediocrity and do something awesome—like just wallop a gorilla and knock him out cold as I was trying to instruct Bob—it's a punch to the face of the hippie inside you. Of course, to be awesome, you don't have to punch a gorilla. Instead you could punch like a moose or a rhinoceros. Or you could do something that doesn't involve punching at all; it just has to be awesome in a mind-blowing way, because that is how you defy that inner hippie telling you lies, like the lie that you're unable to punch out a large charging ape. And when you live a life filled with awesome, then it's like you're constantly curb-stomping the hippie inside you. You do that enough, and he shuts up. And with your inner hippie out of the way, you will be unstoppable. That is our goal.

WHAT IS AWESOME?

People ask me, "What is awesome?"

Usually I answer, "Well, it's not standing around asking dumb questions." When people ask me questions in real life, they're usually interrupting something, and I'm irate and not very helpful. But for this book, at least, I will answer the question.

Webster's dictionary defines awesome as . . . eh, their definition is stupid; never mind that. Awesome is a human being meeting his or her full potential. It is the highest state one can achieve—but not in some boring, enlightened way where you're all peaceful and sit around spouting high-minded ideals that sound okay at first glance but don't make much sense when you really think about them. Like "Imagine world peace"—have you ever tried imagining world peace? It's really boring, and you can never keep it up for more than a couple of seconds before your mind wanders and you think of Hulk smashing people in the *Avengers* movie, which is way cooler to imagine than world peace.

Anyway, when you think of awesome, think of a guy catching a wave from a tsunami while playing a mind-blowing solo on his ax. Think of a guy delivering a flying kick to the face of a *T. rex*, knocking it over, and then whaling on it while yelling, "Don't mess with me, you stupid hippie lizard!"* Think of a guy just walking away calmly while a building erupts into a massive, flaming explosion behind him, and everyone is like, "Don't mess with that guy! He doesn't even care that there is an explosion behind him!"

The people who founded the United States of America are examples of such awesome. They had this great idea for a new country where people were free to be as awesome as they could be, but they had to take on the huge British Empire to make that country happen. It seemed impossible, but they didn't care, because they didn't let hippies talk them down. And thus they kung-fu fought the redcoats, and eventually George Washington put the king of England in a headlock and forced him to sign our Declaration of Independence.†

---

* Technically, *Tyrannosaurus rex* is more closely related to a bird than a lizard, but you don't have to be scientifically accurate all the time when being awesome.

† There may be some embellishment in this story. Some historians say the king of England wasn't in a headlock when he signed the Declaration of Independence but was instead held in check by an angry badger tied to a stick.

Your Inner Hippie Hates Awesomeness

The most important part of awesomeness is that your inner hippie can't stand it.

What is it about awesomeness that makes a hippie—particularly your inner hippie—hate it so much? It's that awesomeness is the opposite of whining. Instead of deciding that the world is out of your control and all you can do is complain until other people fix things for you, you are stepping forward and saying that no matter what the circumstances are, you will achieve things that will astonish and astound those who witness them. You are saying that greatness is in your grasp, and your choices alone decide your fate. So when you make the choice to be awesome, you are taking a brick of determination and smashing it into the face of the whiny hippie inside you.

Also, awesomeness is hard work. Sure, you make it look easy when at your quarterly shareholders meeting you break-dance on the conference table of your multibillion-dollar corporation, but it took a lot of hard work to get to that point. That means that every time your inner hippie told you, "This is too hard. Let's just give up and sleep in today," you said, "Shut up, hippie!" then ripped a pipe out of the wall* and clonked him over the head.

---

* This is metaphorical and in your head, so it's not like you messed up any plumbing by ripping out a random pipe.

Awesomeness is the defiance of all of your inner hippie's messages of failure. Thus your inner hippie will yell the loudest when you set your sights on achieving great and awesome things. And whatever you aim for, no matter how difficult it is—whether it be climbing Mount Everest, becoming a billionaire, or defeating a great white shark in hand-to-hand combat—your biggest challenge will be defeating your inner hippie. Because once that is done, anything is possible.[*]

Awesomeness Is Your Duty as an American

Quick: When I say "America," what do you think of? Probably a bald eagle with a machine gun in its claws gunning down communists, Nazis, and terrorists. The name of this great country always brings to mind awesome things, but how do you fit in there? Your citizenship may say "American," you eat your share of apple pie, and you may even own a flag pin or two, but do you truly represent the awesomeness of America?

---

[*] Some things are still not possible, such as dividing by zero, licking your own elbow, or creating a romantic comedy with a plot that isn't extremely predictable. ("What? The two people who hated each other at the beginning ended up with each other?! What a surprise! Thanks for making me watch this, my dear wife.")

What most people think of when you say "America."

Being awesome not only knocks out your inner hippie, but it also helps you to truly become an American—to represent all that that word describes. As I said, the Founding Fathers were full of awesome and made this country out of nothing more than a pile of dead British people. And then the people who continued to build this country after them were filled with awesome, too. They expanded the frontier, settled the wilderness, grew the economy, and one of them even invented the lightbulb, which I'm pretty sure you use all the time.

So with all the freedoms and technology that Americans worked so hard to make available to you, it's your duty to be awesome as well. You don't have the British standing around, pointing muskets at you, saying, "Don't be awesome, or we'll put an oppressive tax on you." Being awesome should be easy for you, but the obstacle you have left is that inner hippie telling you that awesome isn't for you. He's the one keeping you from being the American you should be, and that is why you need to defy him and be awesome anyway. That is why you *must* punch your inner hippie, or else you spit on everything America has ever stood for, like freedom, nachos, and rattlesnakes that don't like to be trod on.

Awesomeness Myths

Despite how obviously great being awesome is, many people still don't try to achieve awesome because of some misconceptions—many of them planted by the inner hippie. So let's punch those lies with some facts. Let's take on some myths about being awesome.

MYTH: Being awesome is expensive.
FACT: While money can help with being awesome—such as by giving you the ability to afford a hovercraft—you don't

need money to be awesome. Many people have come to this country penniless—and I don't mean they didn't keep change on them because they always used a debit card. These were people with nothing. But they did whatever awesome they could—working hard, helping the community, and winning in underground street fighter matches—until they were pillars of success and could afford their own jet planes. If done right, being awesome will make you money, not cost you.

MYTH: I'll lose many of my friends, as they'll be intimidated by my new awesome.

FACT: Any friends you lose over being awesome probably sucked, and you should be glad you're rid of them. Most of your friends, though, will treat you with a newfound awe and respect when you become awesome. If they don't treat you with awe and respect, get rid of them, too.

MYTH: Only a select few, like Chuck Norris or Mr. T, can be awesome.

FACT: Awesomeness is available to anyone willing to put in the time and effort to grab life by the horns and repeatedly punch it in the face until it admits you are its master. This doesn't take any special skill set, and you aren't born into it. It just takes determination and a willingness to finally punch the inner hippie until he shuts up. And it takes this book. Make sure you have this book. Perhaps have more than one copy, just in case.

MYTH: Ostentatious displays of skill were common in a more primitive time, but there is no place for being awesome in the modern age.

FACT: Today we have a lot of people who, due to the influence of their inner hippies, feel they can't achieve awesome, so they try to make a virtue out of being useless and weak—calling that "civilized." Back in my day we called that "being a sissy"—which is what we also call it in this day. I'm not actually that old; it might still be my day. Anyway, no matter how society evolves, awesomeness will always rule the day, and those who are capable of awesome will be the ones society admires, while those who eschew awesome will be scorned and hated and only allowed to hang out with us if they chip in for gas.

MYTH: Being awesome will be seen by other countries as a form of aggression.

FACT: Well, this one isn't really false; it's just . . . who cares? You're an American reaching his full, awesome potential; other countries should be scared of you.

MYTH: It's the government's job to be awesome, not that of the individual citizen.

FACT: The government is horrible at being awesome and is usually the complete opposite of it. Sure, it did lead the initiative to get a man on the moon, and now, since we got there first and planted our flag on it, America owns the moon, which is pretty awesome. But the government was only motivated to do that because it was up against the commie Soviets (think of what it would be like if a red commie moon shone down on us each night; we'd hate the moon and would want to nuke it, which would actually be a pretty awesome thing to do). Usually the government, with its taxes and regulations and bureaucrats, does nothing but impede awesome. The government is always saying stuff like "Oh, you can't ride a carriage pulled by alligators down a city street; that's against regulations." If we want awesome in this country, it's up to individual citizens, who will most likely have to achieve that awesome in spite of the government.

THE TANK OF AWESOMENESS

So you've gone through it in your head, and you want to be awesome. You're ready to punch and silence your inner hippie by overwhelming him with the sheer brilliance of your greatness. And you're ready to fulfill your destiny by achieving your full potential as an American. But how do you get started? You build a tank.

The tank is widely recognized as the most awesome vehicle in existence. It is an unstoppable armored fortress that can blow up anything that gets in its way. Ask people what vehicle they would most like to drive to work, and they will answer, "A tank." Yeah, some people may answer, "I'd like to drive a hybrid car that's green and will help the environment," but those people are lying. That's just their inner hippies using them to spout nonsense, but even those people, if given the chance, would really rather drive a tank, rolling over Priuses with its massive treads and blowing up trees so they can take a shortcut through the park.

So let's build a tank. But we're not building a physical tank here (though if you have the knowledge and resources to build a physical tank, do that, too, because, man, that will be so cool). Instead, we're going to build a tank out of awesome. You see, I've spent a great deal of my life in the study of awesome. I've gone to numerous demolition derbies. I've watched a lot of kung fu movies. I've witnessed a lion fighting a robot. And I've come to the conclusion that the best way to foster an enduring awesome in yourself is to envision constructing that awesome into a tank.

What your awesome should be.

To do that, you must work on the four essential parts of being awesome that create your tank.

Independence is the treads that allow you to traverse any terrain.

Gratitude is the armor that deflects all problems.

Ambition is the fuel that propels your tank forward.

Confidence is the cannon that blows away any obstacle.

And when you have this tank together, you're going to drive it right into the center of your own brain and institute a regime change. Your thoughts there will probably welcome your invasion with open arms, but if they don't . . . well, you have a tank.

Of course, as with any necessary invasion, the hippie inside you is going to scream and protest. But can a hippie stop a tank? Of course not. A tank is large and invulnerable, and a hippie is small and squishy. When you properly construct your tank of awesome, it will simply roll over your inner hippie if he tries to get in your way. And then you'll stop your tank, jump out, run over to the hippie, and say, "Are you okay?"

And if he says, "Yes," you'll punch him in the face and repeat the question.

So once you have a tank made out of the four essential parts of being awesome, you will be an unstoppable force. Someone others look to in awe and wonder and say, "Now there goes a real American. Someone who is the pinnacle of mankind. Let us cater to his every whim and be thankful for every moment we can bask in his glory." You will radiate so much awesomeness that hippies will punch themselves when they see you.

Are you ready to become this man or woman?

What do you mean, "No"?

Oh, you have to go to the bathroom? Sure, yeah; go ahead. Then we'll start going through each of the four parts of your tank of awesome until you are the—just go. Don't even wait for me to finish this sentence. Your dancing around is distracting.

SUMMARY OF CHAPTER 4: PUNCHING YOUR INNER HIPPIE

In this chapter, we learned:

- You punch your inner hippie by being awesome.
- Awesomeness is meeting your full potential as a human being or something, though it also sounds kind of like being a spaz.
- Awesomeness is obtainable by anyone willing to sucker-punch a gorilla.
- To completely defeat your inner hippie, you must build an unstoppable tank of awesome, because I guess you need a tank to fight a hippie. Kind of seems like overkill.

In the next chapter, we'll look at the treads of your tank of awesome: independence.

Study Questions

Since humans are the only animals known to throw punches, does that help us establish dominance over animals? What have been the results when you've punched various wildlife?

Can you identify some times in your life when you were awesome? Did you feel good about yourself? Did you feel like you were violently attacking some whiny individual deep within you?

Why would some people choose not to pursue awesome? Should you shun these people? Should you punch them?

ANSWERS TO COMMON QUESTIONS

Q. You keep talking about punching hippies in the face. Aren't there other alternatives?

A. Well, the traditional way to handle a hippie is to punch him in the face, as the face is the most annoying part of the hippie. I do know of at least one other way to handle a hippie that doesn't involve punching, though. If a hippie comes at you spouting nonsense, you can try this technique instead of punching:

STEP 1: Put your hands on the hippie's shoulders as if to reassure him.

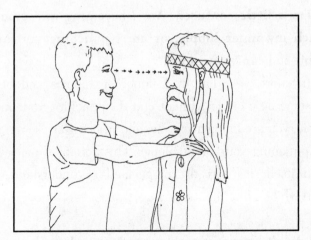

STEP 2: Look the hippie directly in the eyes.

STEP 3: HEADBUTT!

Q. I'm a little confused. Am I becoming awesome to punch my inner hippie, or am I punching my inner hippie so I can be awesome?

A. In short, yes. Think of punching hippies and being awesome as a circle without end. In punching your inner hippie, you are being awesome, and in being awesome, you are punching your inner hippie. This sort of thing layers upon itself; it's sort of complicated to understand, yet worthwhile—like the movie *Inception*.

Q. I didn't have any problem understanding the movie *Inception*.

A. Well, good for you. I'll spin a top in your honor.

Q. A lot of what you describe as being awesome sounds dangerous. Should I have safety concerns when being awesome?
A. No, people should fear you when you're being awesome. When you're awesome, you can just roundhouse kick someone's head off like it's a pumpkin sitting on a fencepost.

Q. But, like . . . punching a gorilla? I can think of at least one thing that can go wrong there.
A. Okay, maybe there is the possibility of harm to worry about, but in the least you'll have a really cool obituary that will inspire others. Also, if you have a family, get some term life insurance. That way if something goes wrong, someone will come to your house and tell your spouse, "I'm sorry, but John Smith died today in one of the most spectacular explosions anyone has ever witnessed. It was pretty much the coolest thing ever. Here's a million dollars."

Q. Insurance companies won't ask if you're trying to be awesome before insuring you?
A. No, they haven't caught on to that yet.

Q. When people were awesome before tanks existed— like the American frontiersmen of old—what personi-

fication of awesome did they make, since they wouldn't know what a tank was?

A. Good question. Maybe like a musket of awesome. I'm pretty sure muskets were the most awesome thing they could visualize in the long, long ago. That or jaunty hats.

Q. Are there other things we should value in life more than being awesome?

A. Gold, maybe.

Q. So what happened to Bob?

A. Who?

5

Independence

I can do it myself!   **—my two-year-old daughter**

I knew this man, Jeremy, who was just a useless lump. "Jeremy, you're disgusting," I told him. "You can't hold a steady job. You still live with your parents. Also, you're ugly, and you're stupid, and there is just this sort of indefinable quality to you I hate and can't stand."

And he said to me, "Who are you?"

"Let's not worry about that. Come with me; we're going to work on changing all that."

"I don't know about this. . . ."

"I have a helicopter."

So we got in my helicopter and took it out into the middle of the wilderness, landing in a clearing.

"So what now?" Jeremy asked.

"We're going to survive on our own out here in the wilderness with nothing but a set of fundamental survival tools like the frontiersmen of old would have had with them," I said. "So a basic rifle, a knife, some camping gear like a small tent, and some matches and such."

"And where are those?"

I shrugged. "I forgot them. So let that be your first lesson: You relied on me to bring survival supplies for you when your survival isn't as important to me as it is to you—and look what happened."

"But you're going to survive out here, too, right?"

"Yep." I got back into the helicopter.

"What are you doing?" Jeremy asked.

"My survival strategy is to take a helicopter out of here."

"How is that being self-reliant?!" he demanded.

"I paid for the helicopter myself. Hey, if you find your own helicopter out here, it's not cheating for you to use it . . . or you can build your own helicopter out of rocks and twigs like something out of *The Flintstones*. Later. Just remember to punch the hippie inside you."

"Punch the what? What are you talking about?!"

So I flew out of there in my helicopter and stayed at a hotel near the forest. Days later, Jeremy emerged from the woods, but now he was a changed man. Or it actually was a completely different man; I'm not really very good with faces, and he was speaking gibberish.

So what was it that changed Jeremy? It was finally learning to be independent.

Now, I ask you: Do people like freedom? No, most people don't. Yeah, sure, if you ask people if they like freedom, they'll always answer, "Oh yeah, I love freedom. Freedom is the best!" That's because they're liars. Little weaselly liars with stupid lying faces. And with dumb lying hats on their heads to keep the sun out of their lying eyes. And shoes on their feet. For walking. Which doesn't have anything in particular to do with lying.

I'm getting distracted.

Anyway, the fact is that most people find freedom too bothersome. Yes, everyone loves the "I get to say what I want, do what I want, eat what I want, watch what I want, make lists of things when I want" aspect of freedom, but there is one part of freedom that most hate dealing with: responsibility.

Responsibility is the other side of the coin of freedom; for anyone who embraces freedom, it is inescapable. When you're a kid, you yearn for the freedom of being an adult, getting to go where you want and do what you want without some parent dictating it all. But when you actually become an adult, you find that the cost of that freedom is getting a job, paying bills, and wearing pants every day. Freedom isn't free, and the cost is responsibility. And many people just don't consider freedom worth that awful price.

But you need freedom if you want to achieve awesomeness. Which means you must also embrace responsibility. And when you have mastered both freedom and responsibility, you are then independent. Our country fought a war for independence, but you just need to beat up your inner hippie to achieve yours—just like Jeremy was forced to when he was alone in the woods.

Independence is the treads on your tank of awesome. When you have independence, nothing can stop you, and you can adjust to any terrain. While others complain about how bad the economy is or that the government isn't fixing things fast enough, you will just roll onward, because you rely on yourself and not other people or external circumstances out of your control. Because if you want to achieve great things, you need to put your fate in the hands of the person most concerned for your well-being: yourself. Now, I have nothing against other people, but let's be frank: They're horrible. They're always worrying about their own problems and not about my much, much more important problems. That's why you never want to rely on other people, and you need to take control of your own life.

Your inner hippie does not want this. Having full control over one's own life is a *huge* responsibility, and hippies recoil from responsibility like a vampire from a cross.* What your inner hippie wants is for you to lounge around in your parents' basement or collect a welfare check while spending all day watching people you don't know buy storage units on TV. Can you meet your full potential in this condition? Of course not; you'll be a loser dependent and a slave to your inner hippie.

But when you exert your independence, you grab your inner hippie and smash his head through a jukebox while yelling, "Shut up! I'm in charge!" And with independence you become a changed man, like Jeremy was after his stay in the woods. You are more powerful. Maybe even a little scary. Perhaps authorities will have to come and tranq you. But whatever. You can now rely on yourself no matter the circumstances, and your awesomeness is truly in your own hands.

So let's put the treads on your unstoppable tank of awesome and learn how to be independent.

INDEPENDENCE'S BIGGEST ENEMY

So what is your biggest obstacle to independence? Friends? Family? No, those are easily overcome. It's the government.

---

* We're talking actual vampires, not the sparkly ones. I don't know what their weakness is; running out of hair gel, I guess.

Back in the day, there used to be plain old oppressive government that considered the citizenry its property. That government existed only to benefit the rulers and would crush all who opposed it. That was nice, because then you clearly understood that the government was your enemy. You'd avoid the government at all costs and join some secret underground movement to amass weapons and plot against the ruling regime, that is, you'd lead a nice, healthy life striving for independence.

But now we have something much more insidious than an openly evil and oppressive government. We have a government that acts like it's there to benefit the people and that everything it does is to help us. And I mean everything. Just think of all the things the government does for us:

- Inspect food quality
- Build roads
- Lock up criminals
- Deliver mail
- Fund scientific research
- Give money and food to poor people
- Fight other countries
- Set health and safety standards
- Read your emails to make sure you're not a terrorist

If a part of you looked at that list and said, "Wow! It's nice that the government does all those things for me!" that would be your inner hippie. That's the part of you you need to hit in the head with a beer bottle. Because the last thing you want to do is to become complacent about the government caring for you, as the government is absolutely horrible at everything it tries to do—except maybe fighting other countries, since that's the one duty of the government where the goal is to destroy things. And destroying things is all the government is good at.

Incompetence and Sociopaths

One advantage of oppressive government is that you might occasionally get someone competent in charge there. Taking over a country might actually appeal to someone who's both ambitious and capable—like a supervillain. In our democratic system of government, that never happens, though. We set up our republic so we'd elect the best and brightest, but those people don't run for office. Instead, the best and brightest build businesses and invent things and create charities to voluntarily help the community, such as one that supplies top hats to homeless people to make them look fancier. So the government is left with people who said to themselves, "I'm not really good at anything, but I'd really like to just get in the way of everyone who actually does know how to be useful and boss them around." Basically, the government is full of incompetent sociopaths. If you didn't know that, then I guess you haven't been paying attention to the news. Get on the Twitters or something, and find out what's going on.

I'm guessing there are a few of you out there saying, "But there are some good politicians." And I have something to say to you. "Shut up; you're an idiot. Please never vote again." Never, ever be so naïve as to like a politician. Let me tell you where I'm coming from. I hate Republicans. Absolutely abhor them. In fact, the only things I hate worse than Republicans are Democrats. I don't subscribe to the magical thinking that these people are going to help me; when I vote, I vote only for who I think will get in my way the least. And if you ever get it in your head that a politician is actually a smart, competent person and is going to fix things, ask yourself this question: "If this guy is such a smart and useful human being, why in the world did he ever decide to run for office?" To give up doing useful work for that shows a nearly psychotic character flaw.

The Only Good Politician

The only politician I'm close to respecting was President Coolidge. Of course, he wasn't even originally elected president and only became one when President Harding died under mysterious circumstances,* because our system is set up to keep sensible people like Coolidge from succeeding in the political world. And what sensible things did Coolidge do? Nothing. Everyone was yelling at him, "You have to do something about the economy and foreign affairs and childhood obesity! Help us, Calvin; you're our only hope!"

And Coolidge was all like, "Meh." In fact, if you went to Coolidge's campaign website—or whatever the equivalent was in the 1920s—I guess like a board with stuff tacked to it or something—and looked under "Issues," "Meh" was his proposed solution for everything. Coolidge used to say, "If you see ten troubles coming down the road, you can be sure that nine will run into the ditch before they reach you and, as for the tenth, why don't you put on your big-boy pants and handle it yourself?"

You see, the problem with any politician in any party is that they're putting all that time and energy into getting into office because they want to do stuff, and stuff is the absolute worst thing any politician can do, as there is nothing our

---

*   I have an alibi.

giant, bloated government staffed by idiots and malcontents won't just make worse. It's a bit like that movie *War Games*: The only winning move is to not play (though, incidentally, I do have a number of winning strategies for nuclear war if anyone is still interested).

Don't Trust Government Solutions

So anyway, government is horrible, and you should never depend on it for anything. For instance, I'd check my own food. I'm not going to blindly trust that Food and Drug Administration; I mean, they're part of the government, so what's their incentive to do it right? Half the country could die from food poisoning, and probably no one there would even get fired. So if you buy some meat, just look it over yourself to make sure nothing is moving on it that shouldn't be. And then put it under a magnifying glass and look for little tubular things. That's *E. coli*—you don't want that.

And know how to build your own roads and bridges, too. Building roads is pretty self-explanatory—you just throw some asphalt on the ground. And a bridge is just a road over water; let's stop acting like that's some spectacular engineering feat.

As for criminals, do you really want the government to handle them? Anyone can grab some guns, put on a costume, and patrol the streets as the Night Avenger, bane of the criminal underworld.

See, you can do a lot of what you depend on the government for yourself, and remember, each time you take on more responsibility, it's like you squeeze harder and harder on the neck of your inner hippie, whom you have in a sleeper hold.

THE ZOMBIE TEST

Right now you may be thinking, "I'm pretty independent." Maybe you have a job and your own place and your own family you're taking care of, but how independent are you, really? Many people these days are more dependent than they realize, so to really check how independent you are, you have to imagine how you would do if the government and most of society disappeared, and a big crisis hit. The traditional scenario for that is a zombie apocalypse.

Imagine you wake up one day and go to check the news on your Twitter feed, but the Internet is out. So you check your smartphone—but you have no bars for your 4G. So you act like it's the olden days and walk to different parts of your house to try to get a signal, but no luck. And then you look out your window and see that the dead are shambling about in the streets. And you're all like, "The dead shouldn't be walking! The dead should be in graves or voting in Chicago. Something is obviously wrong."

And something is wrong. Because of radiation from a crashed satellite or a virus or a curse or something, there are zombies everywhere. And anyone who gets bitten becomes one, because that's how zombie-ism works. And the government has already collapsed, because government employees are the most susceptible to becoming zombies—that's basically what a bureaucrat is.

So what do you do? Well, if you panic and freak out, then you are not an independent individual. Hippies are not going to survive in this scenario; everything is now about survival, with no room for useless people who just annoy everyone and get in the way. Thus those who are really dependent on the government are going to just totally lose it and be like, "We're going to die! Aieee!" Yeah, you will with *that* attitude.

But the independent person is going to say, "Oh. Zombies. Better board up the windows and make sure I have my numerous guns ready. Time for some head shots!" Because the independent person is used to taking care of himself, he's not worried—especially not about some slow-moving creatures lumbering around moaning. Know what's scarier than that? Bears. And the frontiersmen of old used to deal with them all the time. Sure, if you get bitten by a bear, you don't become one—though that would be pretty cool, as now you'd be Bearman with bear powers—but otherwise bears are much more fearsome, and people used to go out all the time into the frontier with no society and no government and deal just fine with the bears.

So, society collapsing because of zombies should be no problem for a true American, as he'll know exactly what to do. First he'll fend off the initial zombie horde and then maybe put on a leather jacket that's missing one sleeve to establish himself as a post-apocalyptic badass. Then he'll get right to work finding a nice place to hunker down, perhaps with room to grow crops and start to rebuild society—but a nicer one with fewer hippies. In fact, a truly independent person would probably prefer the nuisance of a zombie apocalypse to living under government. I mean, you can shoot zombies, and they'll be gone, but government is persistent and everywhere and always coming after you. It's like the Terminator—bulletproof and unstoppable, with a frozen smile on its face as it relentlessly pursues its destructive programmed mission to ineptly help everyone.

Anyway, that is the test of how independent you are: Imagine a zombie apocalypse. If your reaction would be anything other than to shrug indifferently and get to work, you need to work on your independence.

ESSENTIALS FOR INDEPENDENCE

So what do you need in order to be independent? To help out on your quest, I've listed some essentials of independence. If you make sure you're set on everything on this list, you'll be ready for anything. You'll have strong treads on your tank of awesome and be ready to roll over any sort of terrain that lies before you. So here's what you'll need:

Fire: Fire was the first basic tool of man. Well, I guess the first basic tool was probably like a rock, but those are everywhere and hardly worth mentioning. Fire takes a little bit of skill. I know we have lots of modern ways to make fire, with matches and lighters and computer processors we overclocked, but you should know how to make fire with nothing but what you can find in the forest. Then, no matter how bad things get, you'll at least have a nice, warm fire. Plus, I'm pretty sure it's a weakness of zombies if that ever actually comes up.

Guns: Guns are an essential part of being independent, because they mean you are ready to take on criminals, zombies, aliens, communists, and whatever other awful thing life can throw at you. A truly independent person should have his own defense of home and family well under control and not rely on government bureaucrats with guns to come save him if trouble arises. When a knife-wielding maniac busts into your house, would you rather have a phone to call the police or a shotgun? "Oh, hi, police? Yeah, a guy is currently stabbing me. Can you come help? Oh, it will be fifteen minutes? Okay, I'll try not to bleed out by then. Thanks." I'm not saying never use the police; I mean, you can let them remove the dead maniac from your house, because you don't want to touch that, but your day-to-day safety needs to be in your own hands.

Now, your inner hippie will probably protest this and be all, "Oh no! Guns are scary! Keep them away!" When that happens, just work the action on your gun; that sound will scare your inner hippie right away. And other hippie-influenced people might not like your having guns, either, or may question what types of guns you should have, saying things like, "No one needs an assault weapon; those are too dangerous."

Just say to them, "I'm an awesome, independent, law-abiding American; the deadlier I am, the safer everyone else is." And they'll listen to you, because they know you have guns.

Martial Arts: Let's say you're in a tough situation, and the gun gets knocked from your hand. What should you do? Well, pull out your other gun, of course. Why would you have only one gun? That's silly.

But let's say there is a situation where somehow—I don't know how—you don't have any guns. Or maybe you have an enemy you want to deal with nonlethally—like a temporarily deranged puppy. Then you'll need to know basic hand-to-hand combat.

Now, some people are wary of anything called martial arts because it has the word *art* in the title, but this isn't some hippie-type art—this is art that is actually useful, since it's about getting better at hitting people in the face. So not only will knowing some martial arts help you be better prepared for any situation, but it will also improve your hippie-punching skills, making your punches even more educational.

So what's the minimum skill level you should have in martial arts? Well, you are looking for a basic proficiency. That means, if suddenly surrounded by a group of ninjas, you should be able to kung-fu fight them off. I think that's a green belt.

Money: A useful thing to have is money. Money can be exchanged for goods and services, two things you may need from time to time. It can also be exchanged for nachos, ammo, and life-size replicas of Darth Vader—money is just an awesome thing to have. In fact, with enough money, you don't even need all these other skills I'm listing, as you can just pay other people to do them. ("Hey, you. Here's a hundred bucks. Make me a fire.")

Of course, to get money, you'll need some sort of job—the exact sort of thing your inner hippie hates—and to get a good job, you'll have to have some sort of marketable skill. Or often instead of a marketable skill, some companies just want a college degree that pretends you have one. But when getting useful skills, make sure you have the zombie apocalypse scenario in mind. When society collapses, Java programmers aren't going to be in huge demand.

Speaking of society collapsing, it's also a good idea to have some gold. See, right now our money doesn't actually represent anything. A "dollar" is basically just a made-up word we all pretend means something—we could just as easily value everything in unicorn farts. And that's fine, as long as we're all pretending together, but one day someone could go, "Hey, this money here is just imaginary," and then the illusion would collapse, and so would our economy. So that's why you should have some gold as a backup, as it's yellow and shiny, and everyone loves it. Even if our economy withers away, you'll be able to say, "Can you give me some food? Here is something yellow and shiny in exchange."

Just make sure to hide your gold well. I recommend burying it somewhere very remote and then putting directions to it on some sort of well-worn map that you can then hide in a picture frame or something. Then if you die having never needed your gold, some kids in the future can find your map and have a *Goonies*-type adventure recovering it. So, in a way, gold is an investment in children's future.

Trapping Skills: What's something essential you need every day? Air? Well, yeah. That you kind of get for free. Well, I guess plants make it—which makes you kinda dependent on plants. Maybe one day we can make a device that makes air so we'll no longer need plants, because, like most people, you probably hate plants and hate depending on them. They think they're so special, because they absorb the rays of the yellow sun just like Superman, but you're not special, plants. You're stupid.

But anyway, the essential thing you need every day I was trying to get at is food. If you're in a survival situation, do you know how to obtain food? I guess you could forage for berries and stuff . . . if you were a rabbit. But you're a man—or a woman, one of those two—so you need meat. Therefore, you need to know how to wander out into the woods and come back with meat.

This involves making traps like snares and hidden pits with spikes in them (but if you make a hidden pit, make sure to put a sign up to warn people who can read but not tasty animals who can't read). I guess you could also use store-bought traps, but if you're already at the store, you might as well stock up on jerky. You want to make sure you can trap and kill animals with nothing but what you can find in nature. It may seem hard, but really, if you can't outsmart a rabbit, then just give up now. Come on.

Knowledge: What if you don't know something essential to a situation? Well, you just pull out your smartphone and google it. This is a huge advantage we have in the modern age; people of old didn't have Google. Let's say you wanted to know what a honey badger eats. Right now, we just plug "honey badger diet" into Google and get the answer. In days of yore, you'd have to go to a library and consult the card catalog and find a book on African animals and then go locate that book and hope it wasn't checked out and then hope that book has an index telling you where you can find information on honey badgers and then maybe get your answer. It was so tedious, it was better just to remain ignorant.

But you don't want to be dependent on Google. Let's say you try to go to Google and you get a 607 error page, which means nuclear war knocked out the Internet. Uh-oh. Hopefully you already know a lot of essential stuff, since you can't just ask the Internet anymore. So keep reading useful books and articles and fill that squishy thing in your skull with stuff you can know on the ready.

Hey, you're reading a book right now! You're nailing this one. Good job.

Car: A big part of being independent is having transportation. You can walk, but that's tedious and boring. Now there are lots of ways to get around, but the car is the best, because it has a long range and you control it yourself. I mean, if you can own and fly a helicopter, that's awesome, but anyone can get a car. Actually, it's kind of weird in this safety-conscious age where we can't smoke anywhere and they want to outlaw large sodas, that the government still lets absolutely any idiot speed around in a few tons of metal.

Of course, in a situation where society collapses, you'll have to battle roving gangs for gasoline, but if you have the other skills I've listed so far, you should be fine.

Bucket: A bucket is good for carrying things, and when you are independent, you may at times need to carry things. You may also want a wheelbarrow.

AVOID DEPENDENTS

So you've got all the essential skills and are now independent. Despite the protests of your inner hippie, you control your own life and your own fate. Your tank of awesome can take on any terrain by itself. There's a problem: You will now be a target for dependent people. They'll see you, someone who has it all together, and say, "There's someone I can leech off of."

Don't let this happen. If you are to use your independence to continue in being awesome, you must avoid dependents who will sap your ability to be awesome. People will want to "borrow" money from you or crash at your place or have you fight off hordes of bandits for them, but you can't devote your full energy to being awesome when your time and money are going to people who aren't pulling their own weight. If you have someone who is trying to be dependent on you, here's a very kind way to tell them that's not okay:

"Get your sucker off me, you filthy leech."

And then you sprinkle salt on the person's face, because that is how you get leeches off you.

Yeah, so that doesn't sound kind, but the kindest way to deal with people is in a forceful way that makes them confront the hippies inside them that are causing their failures. Also, I don't really get the point of being kind or care to know the point.

I know what you're probably asking now: Since I'm saying you shouldn't have dependents, does that mean you shouldn't have children? No, they are an exception. Yes, every child starts out as a useless dependent sapping your time and money, but in principle there should be a return on this investment. Unlike dependent adults, your children should grow out of it. And if you raise your children right, they will be awesome like you, and then you can declare, "Behold my glorious progeny as they march forth and further conquer this world in my name!" But if for some reason your kids don't turn out awesome and remain dependent, at a certain age you can just kick them out. Yep, when they get old enough, they are no longer your legal obligations. You can just tell them, "I'm sorry, child, but you are a failure. Perhaps it was my fault . . . but more likely it was yours. Bye."

So anyway, you can have children as dependents, but definitely avoid any dependents you don't get a tax deduction for.

So who should be your friends? Well, that should be obvious: other independent people. You only want to be around people who are awesome on their own, but then you can combine all your powers to create even greater things—like with Voltron.

This is especially important in picking a spouse. You definitely only want to marry someone who is awesome like you and will pull his or her own weight. That should be in your marriage vows: "I will pull my own weight."

So if you're a man, you want to marry a strong, independent woman—but not like a screechy feminist who acts all independent but then wants the government to supply everything. They also tend not to find the humor in my ironic misogyny. Hey, lighten up, toots. And if you're a woman, you don't want one of those beta-male, primping and preening types who are all about feelings. Ask your man what his feelings are, and if he answers with anything other than a look of confusion, dump him. A proper man should be too busy for feelings.

As for your friends, it's great for an independent person to have a lot of friends—just make sure they are all of some use to you. For instance, you could have a friend who knows how to do magic tricks. A friend who knows how to do magic might not seem useful now (and he, in fact, might seem a bit creepy), but let's say you and your friends are on a plane and it crashes in the middle of nowhere and are taken prisoner by some primitive tribe, which you then need to convince you're wizards so they'll let you go. Then you'll be all, "I'm glad I have a friend like Archibald."

Oh, I should note that you should make sure you know your friends' names. Friends don't like it when you call them by the wrong name. If you have a particularly large group of friends, instead of remembering all their names, it may be easier to call each one an affectionate nickname based on a physical feature, as that's easier to remember. For example, "Stretch," "Beardo," or "Fatty Fatty Fat Fat."

So go through your list of friends right now and ask yourself about each one: What purpose does this friend serve? If you can't come up with an answer, call that friend up and tell him he can no longer be your friend unless he becomes more useful. You can then helpfully suggest which skill the friend could work on, based on what you lack in your other friends. A good friend worth keeping will respect you for this. A bad friend will respond by cursing at you and accusing you of selfishly exploiting everyone. You don't want a friend like that.

SUMMARY OF CHAPTER 5: INDEPENDENCE

In this chapter, we learned:

- Independence is like the treads on our tank of awesome, because it rotates or something. I dunno.
- Most people lie about liking freedom.
- The government is awful.
- Be ready to fight zombies or something.
- You need a lot of skills to be independent, though money seems like the most important one. The others sound hard.
- Avoid dependents and friends.

In the next chapter, we'll talk about the armor on our tank of awesome: gratitude.

Study Questions

What causes dependence? Is it society? If so, how do we destroy society?

Is there anything the government is good at? Could you

do that better yourself? If not, why do you suck?

Why do zombies hate us?

ANSWERS TO COMMON QUESTIONS

Q. You make it sound like government programs are the opposite of freedom, but isn't part of freedom being free from worries, like whether you'll have enough to eat or have access to health care?

A. Yeah, you know who is free from those worries? A child. Because a child does not understand economics and how those things are supplied and just assumes he gets all the things he wants because he likes them so much. Hey, you can not worry about those things you want and trust some government idiots to get them for you, but eventually the worry will find you when those dimwits fail, and then reality will punch your hippie face harder than I ever could.

Q. Isn't sacrificing some independence part of living in a complex, civilized society?

A. Now, that's your inner hippie talking right there, trying to turn your inability to take care of yourself into some sort of grand virtue. "I'm going to put my fate in the hands of idiots who don't really care whether I live or die because I'm *civilized*. Look at my monocle and bowler hat."

Q. No need to mock me.

A. Well, I can't punch you, so I'm going to mock you, as it's the next best thing to jolt you out of your stupidity. I mean, have you seen politicians and bureaucrats? They're basically like hippies. Would you put your fate in the hands of hippies? I certainly wouldn't, because if they didn't outright break your future or lose it, they'd probably just try to turn your fate into a bong or something. And when you trust the government to take care of you, that's what's going to happen to your future: It's going to end up weird and sticky and gross.

Q. You seem very down on the government. Are you some sort of antigovernment militia type?

A. I just think the government is full of idiots—which is a fact that shouldn't be disputed. Just because you don't like the government doesn't mean you have to be running around the woods with an assault rifle. I mean, I do run around the woods with an assault rifle, but it's for completely unrelated reasons.

Q. You talked about a zombie apocalypse. Is that an actual thing we need to prepare for?

A. I know it seems far-fetched, but people go into mindless, violent states all the time. Just read the comments on You-Tube if you don't believe me.

6

Gratitude

I'm Batman.

—Batman

So I knew this guy named Larry, and he was miserable. "My life is awful," he would say. "I live in a tiny apartment, I have no money, and all my stuff is old and broken."

One day I said to Larry, "Your life is great. And I can prove it to you."

Larry said, "How?"

And then I smiled (people often describe my smile as "creepy") and said, "Just you wait and see. Just you wait and see."

So later that night, I donned a hood and a clown mask and kidnapped Larry from his apartment. After spending a few hours in the trunk of my car, he was transferred to a small cell with no windows and one dim lightbulb. Anytime he tried asking questions, he was doused with cold water from a valve in the ceiling. He was allowed no human interaction and was just given basic food each day, like gruel and water (or, if I felt especially cruel that day, Diet Mountain Dew).

Larry lived this way for two weeks, and then finally I opened the door to his cell and said, "It's over; you can return to your old life."

When he heard this, he cried tears of joy. "Thank you! Thank you!" he cried.

And I said, "Ha! See, I told you your life was great! It's so great that you're now as thrilled to get it back as someone who's just won a hundred million dollars!"

Larry stared at me. "Wait, I know who you are! I know who did this to me!" But he couldn't prove it, because I was wearing a mask and burden of proof and reasonable doubt and all that.

Imagine you suddenly lost electricity and running water. And all gas stations around you ran out of gas. So no phone, no lights, no motorcar—not a single luxury. No Internet or TV, either. So you're going to be like crazy bored. And if there's any particular thing you want to know, hopefully you own a book about it or know someone nearby who has that knowledge.

And now let's say you're hungry. Well, there is no grocery store. You can only get food that has been grown or killed locally—no more bananas imported from across the sea or any of your favorite prepackaged foods. You'll just be lucky to get some unspoiled meat.

This sounds pretty miserable, huh? Well, I just described the lives of most of the richest kings throughout history. Yes, back in the day, people would have given anything to have the advantages of those kings, but now the lives of those kings suck compared to people in the United States we call poor.

Well, I guess kings and emperors could order people around, and you'd probably never get tired of that, but I'd still rather have video games and Google.

Anyway, in this country, every single person has crazy advantages that put us ahead of the richest and most powerful people of just a hundred or so years ago. The life Larry complained about was beyond the wildest dreams of the richest emperors of old. And we were all just given this; we didn't have to work for it. The work was done by the awesome people who came before us, and the fruits of their labor are at our fingertips. See, you stand on the shoulders of giants. And what do you want to do when you are on the shoulders of giants? Of course you want to yell out, "Go, my giant army! Crush and destroy my enemies!" But these giants won't obey just anyone. If you're a whiny hippie, crying, "I wanted taller giants!" the giants will probably just pull you off their shoulders and smash you like a bug. Because the key to controlling the giant armies of the past is gratitude.

Your inner hippie hates gratitude. Because appreciating what you have gets in the way of whining about all the things you think you deserve. If you do not punch out that whiny, entitled SOB inside, you will lead a pointless, miserable life, because no matter what you have, you'll still only focus on what you don't have and then complain about that. Why even go down the path of awesome if you're never going to enjoy it?

But when you master gratitude, it will be the armor on your tank of awesome. No matter what you get hit with in life, you will be grateful for all that you still have and will continue on with a smile on your face. Maybe it will be a creepy smile like mine, which Larry will attest to, but the point is you'll be smiling and unstoppable.

INGRATITUDE MAKES YOU MISERABLE

Right now, list out loud the major problems in your life.

Oh, shut up and stop whining. People don't have problems in this country. We have inconveniences. Problems are things like "I'm going to starve to death" or "Invading hordes are razing my village" or "A crazy guy locked me in a dark, tiny cell." You aren't dealing with anything like that. I mean, what things would people consider major "problems" in today's society?

"I lost my job." Are you going to starve? No? Then shut up. No one cares.

"Gas prices are too high." Do you know what horse prices used to be? And horses could barely get you any distance. And they could bite you.

"I didn't get into the college I wanted." Oh, don't even start, you little whiner.

"I have terminal cancer." Oh . . . well, that one is an actual problem.

Anyway, what you need to realize is that the hippie inside you wants to destroy your joy. That's what happened to Larry; his inner hippie had him so focused on what he thought he lacked that he would never have been grateful for what he had if it weren't for some kindly intervention. In America, we have luxuries that pharaohs would have died for, but no matter how much you have, that whiny hippie inside you only wants to focus on what you don't have. There is no end to this. No matter how rich we are or how great technology becomes, the hippie will do nothing but complain.

"This jetpack is too noisy."

"My robot butler is too curt with me."

"This time portal gave me a headache."

"My spaceship takes a whole hour to get to another galaxy. I need a faster one."

Things that other people would die to have bring you no joy, because you're listening to your inner hippie and his lies about what you deserve. You know what you deserve? Absolutely nothing. No one owes you anything. So you should be extremely grateful for everything you have—just the fact that you won't starve today should thrill you. But you are not happy like that because of the inner hippie and his attack on your gratitude.

INGRATITUDE MAKES YOU FAIL

And it's your ingratitude that is holding you back. Superman didn't have to be this big hero, always saving the day. He could have just spent all day moping around on his couch, whining about things, like, "I wish Lois Lane liked me for me." Isn't it unimaginable that someone with such power—punches that can knock out meteors, super speed, flight, heat ray vision—would just sit around and do nothing with that? Know who that reminds me of? You.

With all of our technology, we basically all have superpowers. We have vehicles that get us from one end of the world to the other in a matter of hours. The Internet brings all the information in the world to our fingertips and allows us to communicate with anyone anywhere instantly. Our phones take pictures and video. We have guns that can kill people at a distance. Whatever superpower you can think of, you have access to tech that basically replicates it. Except talking to fish. So we still need to keep Aquaman around for situations in which communication with fish is essential.*

So if we have all this power, why doesn't everyone just march out each day and totally crush it? Because of that awful hippie inside each of us that wants us to feel powerless. You need to super-punch your own hippie into the sun. Otherwise, you're just Superman vegging out on that couch, never using your powers for anything greater than heating up frozen burritos. I would not read that Superman comic book—sounds too much like some artsy indie crap. Instead, I want a comic where the superhero uses his powers to punch out robot armies, blow up space aliens, and save the world. That's what you need to do. And the first step toward that is learning to be grateful so you can acknowledge all the power you have.

The hippie inside you will resist acknowledging that you are powerful. He wants you to feel sorry for yourself so you can just sit around and do nothing—nothing being a hippie's favorite thing to do. You could be a billionaire with plenty of money to pay for an underground cave and buy gadgets for your utility belt, but that hippie inside you will still say, "You

---

*   Such a situation has never happened but is theoretically possible.

lost your parents as a kid; you have it rougher than anyone else. Why don't you send Alfred to get you some Cheetos so you can just mope around."

That hippie is your Kryptonite, sapping away your power. So you have to punch him out, and you do that with gratitude.

THE PUNCH OF GRATITUDE

One of the best ways to shut up the whiny hippie inside you trying to drag you to failure is with gratitude. Every time you are genuinely grateful for your advantages and your circumstances, it's like picking up a brick and smashing it into the face of your whiny inner hippie.

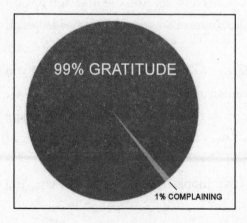

99% GRATITUDE

1% COMPLAINING

Optimal Gratitude

Versus Complaining

Now, am I saying you can never, ever complain? Not quite, but I think this chart does a good job showing the optimal level of gratitude versus complaining.

So you should be grateful about most everything, because, being an American, you live a very privileged life. There's just a tiny amount of room for complaining, because there are a few legitimate things worth complaining about. Like, let's say you watched a show about people who crashed on an island, and it was full of interesting mysteries, and you kept watching for six seasons, hoping to find answers to all the mysteries—but then in the finale they totally didn't answer anything and acted like it was the characters and their resolutions I was supposed to care about—like Jack's constant whining should have been my focus rather than the smoke monster or the mysterious hatch. That's awful. That's worth complaining about . . . even years later.

But other than that, you mainly should just be grateful. So how do you improve on your gratefulness? I have some techniques to share for that (about which you should be grateful).

Be Grateful Here and Now

We have tons of things to be grateful for in our lives, but too often we overlook them. So let's take some time to just be grateful for what's around us right this instant. For example, there's this book in front of you. Books and literacy used to be quite rare. To write anything down, people used to have to kill a giraffe and tan its hide to make parchment and then stab a squid with a small stick to get ink. You were lucky if you had one thing to read in the house, and it was probably just some ancient nonsense about how the earth is resting on the back of a turtle—things today's science has almost disproven. Now, though, there are thousands and thousands of books you can buy anywhere—you can even download countless books to a little electronic device. Also, books used to be really boring, but then I started writing them.

See, these are all things you should be hugely thankful for, but they're things we actually have to stop and think through to realize how lucky we are. And there are countless other things around you right now you should be thrilled to have. Like are you sitting on a chair or a couch? People didn't always have things like that. They used to have to sit on stumps or rocks with no nice, fancy cushioning. Your life is so much more comfortable than that. Are you wearing pants? Do you know how long man went without inventing pants? I mean, for the longest time, no one had pants. It was ridiculous. But you probably have like two or three pairs. Pants are awesome. Just think of all the things you can do while wearing pants.

And you can be thankful for so much more than just our technological advances; you can also find lots of things out in the middle of the woods that are cool to have. Like trees, the sky, air, grass, moss—well, I guess I don't really care much for that last one—but you get the idea. You should also be thankful that you have this solid planet below. A lot of planets aren't solid but are gaseous. If you lived on one of those planets, you would fall right through and choke on all the gases—most of which aren't healthy. So it's pretty cool that you have this nice, solid planet Earth below you—even though Mars is arguably a better planet.

This is an exercise you should do multiple times per day. No matter where you are—the emergency room, a Turkish prison, Detroit—you should be able to find a few things around you to be thankful for. You probably shouldn't do this exercise when you're in a really dire situation, though, like when a lion is charging you. Actually, there's one more thing you can be grateful for: There's no lion charging you. Back in the long, long ago, lions were everywhere and constantly charged people, but you don't have to worry about that as much, because I guess we killed most of them . . . probably because all that getting-charged-by-them was pretty annoying.

The Caveman Test

Whenever you feel like complaining about something, here's a quick way to put things in perspective. I want you to imagine a caveman—someone who has lived a hard life on the edge of survival with no modern conveniences beyond precious fire—a fire that took him an hour to start because he could only do it by rubbing two sticks together and couldn't even do that battery trick the Boy Scouts teach. And now I want you to explain your "problem" to this caveman and imagine what he would think of it.

"I've looked everywhere, and I can't find my cell phone charger."

"I have to get the seat warmer on my car repaired again."

"My cat vomited on the bed."

Do you think the caveman—still out of breath from running from a saber-toothed tiger when he was out collecting berries—would appreciate any of your whines? No, he'd probably just become angry at you and your gibberish and then club you over the head—the primitive version of a hippie-punch. So any time you think about whining, just think of the caveman hitting you in the face with a tree branch. That will give you proper perspective.

Travel the World

Have you ever been to other countries? They are, for the most part, the worst things ever. Citizens of countries other than the United States often live with brutal oppression, famine, disease, and French people. And that's just Canada. It gets worse the farther you get from America. I'm not necessarily complaining—without some despotism and rampant poverty, Chinese-made iPhones would cost like fifty dollars more a pop—but when you see how things are in other countries, it makes you appreciate all the freedoms and advantages we have in this one. Do you know there are countries where the per capita income is less than a thousand bucks? You could be the laziest beggar and get way more money than that on the streets here. Yeah, you might get punched by me for being a hippie, but there are things much worse than punching that happen to people in some of those hellholes out there.

So that's why I recommend traveling the world. Doing that, you can learn a lot about other nations' cultures—though I don't recommend that. Other cultures are stupid and are a big reason why the countries that have them are so awful. Instead, you should just sort of gawk at how horrible everything is for foreigners. When you see how miserable things are in other countries, it will help you have gratitude for all the advantages you have here. You'll be walking around those countries, saying, "This is awful. I can't believe people actually live like this. How do you people not just kill yourselves?" Sure, it's rude, but rude tourists are just another reason living in other countries is the worst.

AWESOMENESS IS YOUR DUTY

There's one more thing that goes along with being grateful. When you look at all the technology and advantages you have in America, you should realize that not only is awesomeness a possibility for you, but it is, in fact, your duty. Our forefathers didn't shoot British people, beat up wildlife, and strangle communists just so we can all be a bunch of losers moping around and accomplishing nothing. They wanted to lift us up so we can achieve even greater levels of awesome. And thus being awesome is the ultimate way we show gratitude.

So whenever you are okay with being average, you have just dishonored all that America stands for and ungratefully cursed the gifts given you by those who made this country. It's like you put on a red coat and started shooting at the Founding Fathers while shouting, "I love punitive taxes on tea!" But you are thanking those who came before you by being awesome and conquering your inner hippie. So when you push your inner hippie down a flight of stairs, you're saying, "Thank you for this country and all the advantages I have by living in it." And then you go down the stairs, find your mangled inner hippie, and kick him some more, because he was making noise. I don't know if that action in particular shows gratitude, but the point of this book is to keep beating up on your inner hippie, so just keep doing it.

SUMMARY OF CHAPTER 6: GRATITUDE

In this chapter, we learned:

- Gratitude is the armor of your tank of awesome because . . . well, I don't really get that.
- We'll whine about really cool stuff in the future.
- Superman moping around is boring.
- You can punch your inner hippie by being thankful . . . a really violent thankful, I guess.
- Pants are great.
- If you complained to a caveman, he would hit you on the head with a rock.
- Other countries suck.
- If you're not awesome, you get a red coat.

In the next chapter, we'll focus on the fuel of your tank of awesome: ambition.

Study Questions

Is it worth giving your kids a better life if, like everyone else, they'll just be ungrateful for it?

Is it wrong to hope the answer to that first question is "No" so you can save a lot of money?

What superhero would you most want to be? If you didn't say Aquaman, how would you handle a situation in which you needed to talk to fish?

ANSWERS TO COMMON QUESTIONS

Q. Now I'm getting really confused. First you said I needed to be awesome to punch my inner hippie . . . but also sort of said I needed to punch my inner hippie to be awesome. And now you're saying being awesome is the best way to show gratitude . . . which you say is a key to being awesome. This is getting so circular. You're basically saying the key to being awesome is being awesome. A. Exactly.

Q. You say everyone should be grateful, but what do you say to someone who was born without hands, was orphaned, had his house burn down and his puppy run over, and now somehow got leprosy?

A. Walk it off.

Q. You mentioned superheroes quite a bit in this chapter, so I was wondering who you think would win in a fight between Superman and the Hulk?
A. Superman. He'd just punch the Hulk into the sun.

Q. Would Superman really just kill the Hulk like that?
A. What am I? His parole officer? He can do what he wants.

Q. Who would win in a fight between Superman and Aquaman?
A. Aquaman.

Q. Um . . . really? I was just joking on that question. Who would ever pick Aquaman?
A. I'm telling you, Aquaman would win. He would lead Superman deep under the water, where Superman is weakest (less sunlight, from which Superman gets his powers), and then pummel Superman until Superman drowned.

Q. Superman can drown?
A. Does he look like he has gills?

Q. Well, what if Aquaman has to fight Superman on land?

A. Then Aquaman would just beat Superman to death with a crowbar made out of Kryptonite.

Q. Why would Aquaman have a crowbar made out of Kryptonite?
A. Well, if there was this guy flying around acting like he's all that and you knew his weakness was Kryptonite, wouldn't you carry around a crowbar made out of that, just in case?

Q. Wouldn't the Hulk then win a fight with Superman using the same method?
A. No, you're being stupid. The Hulk is from the Marvel universe, where there is no such thing as Kryptonite, so it would make no sense for the Hulk to ever have a Kryptonite crowbar.

Q. This whole thing with you thinking Aquaman would win in a fight with Superman makes me question your wisdom in the rest of this book.
A. Hey, I'm giving you the right answers—maybe not the ones you're expecting, but they're backed up by facts and logics and lots of comic books I've read.

Q. I was going to try your tip of imagining telling my problems to a caveman, but there's just one issue: A caveman wouldn't know English.
A. Then just imagine he knows English.

Q. But if he knows English, that would probably mean he's been exposed quite a bit to this modern world and thus won't be as perplexed by our modern problems.

A. Well, let's just say a time traveler went back in time and taught the caveman English . . . while showing him nothing else from this world.

Q. Who is the time traveler who did that?

A. Um . . . I dunno . . . uh . . . Doctor Who.

Q. Doctor who?

A. Exactly.

Q. What?

A. Huh?

Q. Who is the doctor?

A. Yes, the doctor is Who.

Q. You want me to tell you the doctor?

A. I told you the doctor.

Q. Who?

A. Yes.

Q. Wait, are you talking about the BBC series *Doctor Who*? I think the protagonist from that is just called "the Doctor."

A. First base.

Q. Huh?

A. You threw off my rhythm on this.

7

Ambition

I'm bored. I think I'll go someplace new today.

—Christopher Columbus

So I knew this woman named . . . Jill, I guess. Anyway, she was all excited, because she was going to start her own business. And I said, "Great. Starting your own business is a powerful, American thing to do. Andrew Carnegie started his own business. Steve Jobs started his own business. And look where they are now. Well . . . dead, I guess. But their businesses are still around. But know who didn't start his own business? Adolf Hitler."

She just stared at me silently for a moment. My ideas can take time to absorb.

"So what kind of business are you starting?" I asked.

"A bakery," she answered, smiling.

I waited for her to continue her explanation, but she didn't, so I prompted, "A bakery that does what?"

"Well . . . bake things. Like bread and cakes."

I still didn't get it. "Bread and cakes that do what?"

"Um . . . they don't do anything except be delicious."

"You're not going to make a robot out of bread or some sort of hover cake that doesn't require a plate because it hovers?"

Jill looked confused. "No."

"So this is just going to be some boring, stupid bakery like you can already find anywhere?"

"Well . . . no. I'm going to make my bakery the best—"

I went ahead and interrupted her, as it was obvious by now that she was wasting my time. "Your idea of opening a bakery is stupid and worthless and an insult to this great country. And you are stupid and worthless for pursuing it."

Jill then started crying. What is it with women and crying?

Anyway, my point that I would have explained to Jill if she hadn't run off (I really have a problem with people running off before I get to the point) was that in America, we need to aim high. And I mean really high. So high that people say, "You can't actually hit something that high. The bullet will lose momentum before it reaches the target and fall back down and hit you in the head." But that's just your inner hippie trying to discourage you. Or it's actual people around you. Either way: punching.

Because what does the Declaration of Independence say is one of our fundamental rights? The pursuit of happiness. And that's what you need to do: You need to find some happiness and pursue it. That happiness must possess your wakeful mind, and then you need to stalk, kill, and skin that happiness.

Oh, you're already happy, you say? Shut up. Find some new happiness and hunt that down. You must always have new happiness quarry to pursue. You must be bloodthirsty for happiness, never satisfied with whatever happiness you obtain, and always moving forward. This is ambition. For your tank of awesome, ambition is your fuel. It is what drives you to do great things, constantly pushing forward to get to each lofty goal you've set your sights on. You must continually fill your tank of awesome with ambition to keep it always moving. That means that as soon as one of your ambitious goals becomes attainable, you need to set an even greater one. The only complacency you will ever have will be death.

Your inner hippie, in his mission to destroy your awesomeness, will of course fight against this drive. You may say, "Today I'm going to invent a new product, build a business, overthrow a dictatorship, and karate-chop a rattlesnake!" but your inner hippie will say, "Man, that sounds hard, and it's probably not going to work out. Let's just play some Grand Theft Auto." Whenever you set your sights high, he'll try to readjust your aim down to low, easily obtainable things that provide you with no awesome. So what do you have to do to fight your inner hippie on this?

That's right! You punch him in the face! You've been paying attention to this book.

And the way you punch that noisy, useless hippie is with an uppercut of ambition. Your hippie would be happy if you just sat around on welfare watching reality TV all day, but you need to smack that hippie in the face with your big plans and your declaration that you will not be satisfied unless your life is a constant cavalcade of challenges, riches, and explosions.

AMBITION MADE THIS COUNTRY

Were the founders of America ambitious? Well, if they'd listened to their inner hippies, they would have said, "Oh, I guess we can just pay the unreasonable taxes to the British. I mean, what's the alternative? Grab some muskets and start a war? That's like impossible. Let's just play some hacky sack." But the Founding Fathers did not listen to their inner hippies. Instead, they shot lots of British people.

And ambition was what drove the frontiersmen out into the wilds. Their inner hippies were like, "You can't go out there; you'd be on your own! If you got thirsty, your mom wouldn't be there to get you a juice box! And the place is full of wild animals! And not fun animals like the ones from the circus that ride unicycles and juggle; we're talking mean ones that bite and are overly antagonistic when you try to teach them juggling or any other basic clowning skills!" But the frontiersmen just punched those hippies inside themselves and ventured into danger anyway, because they were fueled by ambition and thus ready to go forward no matter what challenges, obstacles, or non-entertainment-minded wildlife they faced.

Everything you have now—from your freedoms to your technology to the readily available burgers and fries on every street corner—is because of the ambition of those who came before you. People who looked at things as they were and said, "This could all be better. We can have a greater country with more freedom. Electronic boxes should be in everyone's house and interconnected so we can share thoughts 140 characters at a time. And I'm tired of waiting up to an hour for good food; I want mediocre food within minutes." But instead of just whining for things to be better—the inner hippie's only response to such grand ideas—these people had the ambition to make the changes themselves. Because when you have ambition, you just punch that inner hippie as soon as you see him—before he can even get a word out. Because you have a world to change.

And since you have all these great things because of the ambition of those before you, what is expected of you? Well, your inner hippie would say, "You should just lie back and enjoy all the stuff others did for you while complaining loudly and annoyingly about it." Should you listen to him?

I hope you didn't answer that question, because it was rhetorical. And if ambition is driving you, you don't have time to waste on pointlessly answering rhetorical questions (because, come on, who would be this far into this book and say, "Yes. I should listen to my inner hippie"? I mean, really).

What you should do instead of listening to your inner hippie is set your sights even higher. If the efforts of those before you got you this far, then you need to have the ambition to do things much greater than they did. The greatest results of the hard work of the best and brightest of those who came before you is now your floor. Because of your advantages, everything you do should make all their efforts look like a bunch of garbage babies would do. That's the level your ambition should aim for to bust your inner hippie right in the chops.

THE AWESOME, TRANSFORMING
POWER OF AMBITION

So what do you use your ambition for? Answer: Everything. Using ambition, you can transform a normal, everyday goal into something awesome. Because if you're doing anything and not aiming for greatness, it's not going to give you that drive to keep your tank of awesome rolling on.

Here are some examples of using ambition to turn boring goals into goals that are worth your time:

Regular Goal: Cook a nice meal.

After Ambition: Cook a meal so great that it changes people's lives and they vomit at the thought of eating a meal not cooked by you.

Regular Goal: Be a good parent.

After Ambition: Have your family become a dynasty that dominates the political climate in the realm like a house from *Game of Thrones.*

Regular Goal: Get a promotion at work.

After Ambition: Have your work overturn the entire

industry, revolutionizing society. Spend your free time basking in the adulation of the press and swimming in your big vault of money.

Regular Goal: Take a nice picture of the moon.

After Ambition: Take a picture of a nuke going off on the moon.

Regular Goal: Get involved in local politics.

After Ambition: Become such a huge local influence that the town is renamed after you.

Regular Goal: Save for retirement.

After Ambition: Discover the secret of eternal youth and never retire.

Regular Goal: Get a good education.

After Ambition: Master every field of study and every skill to the point that you make Batman look like some poser.

Regular Goal: Get that raccoon out from under the house.

After Ambition: Become a raccoon-killing machine such that you are known as the "Raccoon Bane" and are a fearsome legend among raccoons, spoken of among them only in hushed whispers.

Regular Goal: Clean up the yard.

After Ambition: Make a yard so beautiful that random passersby will knock on your door and hand you money because they just assume there is some sort of fee to look at it.

Regular Goal: Get exercise and save money on gas by bicycling to work.

After Ambition: Forget about exercise and saving money and instead jetpack to work, because everyone will be in constant awe of that awesome guy who just jetpacked in to work while a guy on a bicycle looks like a dork.

APPLYING AMBITION

So now you're probably saying, "I want to unleash the power of ambition and knock out my inner hippie with the punch of awesomeness." Well, good; you're now ambitious about ambition. But your next question probably is, "But where do I start?"

In the previous chapter, I asked you to look around and see everything through a lens of gratitude, taking in all the blessings you have. Now I want you to look around with the eyes of ambition. I want you to look around and see the flaws in everything—think about how each thing around you can be improved. For instance, I noticed that the bookstore just doesn't carry enough books about punching hippies. Once you find things that can be improved, begin to plot how to do it. If it helps, imagine yourself sitting in a command center inside a hollowed-out volcano—the traditional place for such grand scheming.

But plotting how to make the world around you more awesome is only the first part of ambition. You also need a real plan of action and follow-through. This is where you will need to focus on only a few ambitious goals, because you don't have time to be awesome at everything.

Ha! I'm kidding. That was a test. If you were truly tapping your ambition, you would have responded to my telling you what you can and can't do with a shout of "Bah!" and a dismissive wave of your hand. True ambition defies all constraints people would dare try to impose on it.

"Oh, you can't put a man on the moon. That's crazy!"

"A personal computer in everyone's home? Who would need such a thing?"

"A taco where the shell is a big Dorito? That is an affront to both God and man!"

What can I say? Don't listen to people; people are stupid.

Anyway, if you're properly applying your ambition, your lazy inner hippie should be whimpering at the thought of the Herculean tasks you have set before yourself. Maybe he'll even start screaming at you to stop and reconsider such huge undertakings. And that's when you pour your ambition into your tank of awesome and just run him right over. No screams or pleas or cries for rationality will stop you, because ambition keeps you moving forward. All objections will be little crunching sounds under your treads.

So what have you seen around you that could be made more awesome? What in your life can you improve? What grand, insane schemes can you come up with? It's time to crush your inner hippie and lunge after these grand new ideas, embracing the ambition that is your American heritage.

Let's set a couple of goals right now.

GOAL SETTING

To really start achieving things, you need a concrete set of goals. Not vague things like "I want to be happier" or "I want a more fulfilling family life" or "I want to read more intelligently written books." Those are stupid, and how do you know if you achieve them? They are the sorts of goals your inner hippie will try to set. Haven't you punched him enough yet? Why is he still conscious to give you suggestions?

Instead, you need measurable goals so you know when you have succeeded. That way, you can actually celebrate your successes with a cake or by firing a gun in the air* or blowing up a beached whale with dynamite—however you like to celebrate things. And as you achieve one goal, you know to move on to the next one—to keep your tank of awesome rolling toward new things to conquer.

So let's set those goals. To start, let's make some long-term ones. Think of yourself twenty, thirty years from now (if you're really old, you can skip this step). Where do you want to be then? Make some long-term goals, and make sure they are concrete and measurable. Not "I want to own a big business," but instead "I want to own a multibillion-dollar company that makes cakes that hover, completely revolutionizing how we eat, since we'll no longer need plates." (Wow, that was a good idea Jill had; I don't know why she didn't run with it.) So write down your long-term goal.

Now rip up that goal and toss it out. It wasn't ambitious enough, you little twerp.

I mean it: You need real ambition here. I want giant, seem-

---

* I should mention that proper gun safety says you shouldn't fire a gun in the air since the bullet will eventually come back down at high speed, so if you must fire a gun in the air, make sure you do it someplace near no one you know or care about, and make sure to vacate the area soon afterward.

ingly crazy goals. If you're doing it right, your inner hippie will be yelling at you that there is no way you'll achieve it. And then you'll punch him back by making the goal even more ambitious than the one he objected to. When you've beaten your goal over the head of your hippie so much that he finally shuts up, that means you're now where you should be.

So now you need shorter-term goals to help lead you to this long-term goal. Like a goal five years out. For instance, if your long-term goal is to become president of the United States ten years from now, start with an easier goal of becoming president of Canada five years from now. Then you need an even closer goal, like one to achieve in one year. And then one month. Then a goal to achieve by the end of the week. Then the end of the day. And finally, to get started, you need a goal to achieve right this moment. The sooner you start achieving ambitious goals, the more beating you'll be giving the hippie inside you, so let's start with an uppercut right now and find something ambitious you can achieve this moment. Perhaps actually write out your goals since I bet you've just been reading and not writing down goals like I told you to.

So now you have a list of goals—short-term and long-term—to work toward. This is the fuel for your tank of awesome—it will continue driving you forward at breakneck speed, rolling over doubt, mediocrity, and hippies. And you should have only one set of goals that leads to one long-term goal, as anything else will be a distraction.

If you nodded in agreement with that, you're an idiot. I just tricked you again; you should have numerous long-term goals, each with its own set of shorter-term goals. You're trying to be awesome here, and that means achieving on all fronts. Plus, when you have enough goals, you can just constantly achieve them.

Boom! Your company just made the Fortune 500 list, you were the first person to land on Mars, and you got the gold medal in curling. That's what every day should be like for you.

You will be a goal-achieving machine. Goals will flee from you, as you're just blowing them away left and right, but they won't be able to run for long, as you'll be chugging along in your giant tank, running on high-octane ambition. And you will sit there laughing, the blood of goals smeared all over you.

TIME MANAGEMENT

How much time do you have left on Earth? You don't know. Tomorrow a koala could fall out of a tree and land on your head, and you'd be dead. Time is a finite resource, and as part of ambition, you need to make sure you put your time to great use and don't waste it. Every minute of every day, you have to ask yourself, "Am I doing something awesome right now?" And if the answer is no, you need to stop what you are doing and put your time to better use. Unless what you're doing is sleeping, which is never really "awesome" per se but still quite necessary.* But other than that, you need to make sure you are tapping into your ambition and using your time to achieve great things, because when you waste time, it's gone forever.

Goldilocks and the Three Bears

Let me tell you a story. There is a house in which live three bears—a papa bear, a mama bear, and a baby bear. They have just made themselves some porridge and decide to take a walk while it cools. They exit their house, but they don't lock the door since, you know, they're bears—they don't know how to work a lock. I'm not even quite sure how they got a house or learned to make porridge.

Anyway, while the bears are away, a girl named Goldilocks sneaks into their house. I'm not sure why she randomly breaks into houses; maybe she's a troubled youth. She has a bad home life. Is possibly a gang member.

---

* Scientists say you'll die without sleep, but they could have just told their supervisors that so they could get away with napping on the job.

So she sees the three bowls of porridge and decides to eat some. First she tries the papa bear's porridge, but it's too hot—and she's not about to stand around waiting for it to cool after she's broken into someone's house. Next she tries the mama bear's porridge, but it is too cold (I guess it was the porridge that was microwaved first). Finally, she tries the baby bear's porridge, and it's just right. So she eats it all up. Usually, you'd think kids these days wouldn't be all enthused about porridge, but remember: Goldilocks is a thug. It's not about the food so much as the thrill of eating stolen porridge.

So now Goldilocks is a little sleepy. So she heads upstairs to find the beds. I know what you're thinking: Goldilocks isn't exactly a criminal mastermind here; you don't break into someone's house and then go to sleep unless you want to get caught. But maybe she does want to get caught. Maybe this is all a cry for help.

Anyway, she tries the papa bear's bed, but it's too hard— and it's not one of those Sleep Number beds you can adjust. So she tries the mama bear's bed—the papa and mama bears don't sleep in the same bed anymore, as they're having some trouble, but that's a completely different story—but the bed is too soft. So Goldilocks tries the baby bear's bed, and it's just right. And she falls asleep.

So the three bears arrive back home. The papa bear looks at his porridge and says, "Someone has been eating my porridge." And if you're wondering how he can tell someone took just one bite, well, he's a bear, and bears have better senses than you or I.

The mama bear looks at her porridge and says, "Someone has been eating my porridge."

And the baby bear looks at his porridge and says, "Someone has been eating my porridge and ate it all up!"

Now, you or I would call the police at this point, but they're bears, and they don't like to get the authorities involved, as they've had bad experiences with animal control in the past. So they go upstairs to investigate. The papa bear sees his bed and says, "Someone has been sleeping in my bed." (I guess they made their beds in the morning; these must be well-trained circus bears or something.)

The mama bear looks at her bed and says, "Someone has been sleeping in my bed."

The baby bear looks at his bed and says, "Someone has been sleeping in my bed, and there she is!"

Goldilocks hears the baby bear shout and wakes up to see three angry bears staring at her. The papa bear yells, "Who are you? And how'd you get in here?" Except he's saying it in bear language, so it's just a bunch of growls to Goldilocks, and she is like freaking out. She screams and pulls out her Glock and starts firing at the bears, but she has no formal firearms training and holds the gun that stupid sideways gangster-style way and totally misses the bears. Plus, they're bears; they're not going to be scared of a 9 mm. So Goldilocks just jumps out the window—smashes right through the windowpane—there's glass everywhere. But she lands on the ground with enough wherewithal to get to her feet and just run. And maybe now she's been scared straight from her criminal ways, because bears will do that to you.

So what's the point of this story? The point is that there is no point! I had just talked to you about time management and how important your time is, and yet you just sat there as I wasted your time and told you a story you've heard a million times already. You could have used that time to start a business, write a novel, or master the touch of death, but you lacked the ambition to use your time more efficiently. Now that time is gone forever. So I hope you really liked that umpteenth retelling of "Goldilocks and the Three Bears," because you basically just ruined your life by reading it.

No, not really, but that's how you need to think of your time; it's this precious resource of which you have only a limited amount. The hippie inside you wants you to be just fine sitting around and completely wasting it as you achieve nothing in life, but you need to have the ambition to put your time to great use.

So should you never watch TV or play video games or anything else that uses up your time? Of course not; video games are fun and awesome, and there's some great TV, like *Breaking Bad* (I haven't actually seen that show, but everyone raves about it). When you work hard, you should have some time to enjoy yourself, but the key is you first have to work hard (take that, inner hippie) and make sure you use the time on stuff you actually enjoy. If you start to not enjoy a video game, stop playing it. Ask yourself: Are you still launching birds at green pigs because you're having fun or out of a misplaced sense of duty? And if you're not enjoying a TV show, stop watching it. Don't go, "Well, I need to clean space off the DVR, so I'd better watch it." Just stop DVRing shows you don't actually enjoy. And don't let someone tell you, "Oh, this show is great, but it doesn't really find its footing until the third season." Demand that shows be good from the get-go, or don't watch them. Don't let video games or TV shows or anything else waste your time. Be the guy who walks out in the middle of a movie. If you have the ambition to demand excellence from your work, demand excellence from your free time as well.

STRESS

You often hear you should avoid stress, but should you really? Do you know what doesn't have any stress? A rock. A sack of potatoes. The dead.

Stress is just your body's way of saying, "Hey, shouldn't

you be doing something right now?" And your body is right: You should be doing something, because when you stand around doing nothing, you're just one bindle away from being a hobo. Now, your inner hippie will want you to avoid stress by never having the ambition to achieve anything, but you will never find peace down the hippie's path, because eventually you will be consumed with the stress of being a lazy, filthy hippie whom everyone hates.

Stress is just the part of ambition that actually makes sure you're on the move and accomplishing things. When you set lofty goals, you're going to place a lot of stress on yourself to actually reach those goals. So how do you relieve this stress? Well, you know how your inner hippie wants you to handle things. "Well, I can't raise a family, train for a mixed martial arts tournament, breed prizewinning emus, work on my rap album, hunt for Al Qaeda terrorists, and teach cats to do circus tricks all at the same time; it's too stressful. I'll just try to achieve less. Oh, sweet mediocrity—hold me in your flabby embrace!"

But the best way to relieve stress is to accomplish things. Like, let's say you're stressed about finances. So go become a billionaire. Boom; no more stress on that front, and you're awesome.

Of course, if you achieve enough, you'll soon have so little stress that you'll start to become a lazy hippie, which is why you have to keep adding new goals to give yourself new stress to keep active. You just need to strike a balance; you want to stoke the fire of stress inside you enough to keep yourself moving but not so much that it eventually overtakes your body, burning you out from the inside until you are a hollow husk of a man. You don't want that. So some stress but not too much. If it kills you, that was too much.

SUMMARY FOR CHAPTER 7: AMBITION

In this chapter, we learned:

- Bakeries are stupid.
- You need ambition to fuel your tank, because apparently it's not battery powered. I don't know if they make hybrid tanks.
- Ambition can turn simple, useful activities into crazy, lunatic things.
- You need to write out goals that are long-term, short-term, and medium-term. It sounds like a lot of work.
- Some of the stories Frank tells might be tricks. Don't read them.
- If you are not stressed, you are potatoes.

In the next chapter, we'll talk about the cannon on your tank of awesome: confidence.

Study Questions

What causes some people to be satisfied with mediocrity? Do you think Satan is involved? Or Democrats?

When people don't write out goals, do they even know what they are trying to achieve? Or do they just kind of piddle around until their DVRs record something interesting?

Think of the last time you had a really stressful day. Did you take the stress head-on by trying to accomplish something, or did you curl into a ball and whimper? Which do you think is the more effective strategy?

ANSWERS TO COMMON QUESTIONS

Q. Doesn't this chapter contradict the last? In the previous chapter, you said we had to learn to be grateful for all we have, but in this chapter you want us constantly trying to achieve more than what we have.
A. Being grateful for what you have doesn't mean you can't constantly strive to have more. Stop trying to make this complicated.

Q. It just seems like you're tasking us with dual purposes—both looking for contentment and trying to improve our lot in life.

A. I already dismissed your silly concern. Shut up.

Q. Don't we need some people to be nonambitious and be janitors and fry cooks and run regular bakeries, or nothing would get done?
A. Yes, but that's what other people are for. There will always be many mediocre people in the world, but I assume you bought this book because you want to be awesome. Otherwise, instead of this book you would have picked up *Settling: How to Not Be So Disgusted with Your Pathetically Average Life.*

Q. Is that an actual book?
A. If it isn't, I probably should write it, because a large segment of the population really is mediocre, and if I wrote a good book aimed at them, I could totally clean up.

Q. You'd probably want a less insulting title.
A. Why are you brainstorming about it? Are you thinking of stealing my idea? If you do, I'll murder you.

Q. You can't just threaten to murder someone like that.
A. Yes, I can because of the Castle Doctrine. A man's book is his castle, and thus you can threaten to murder someone from within the confines of it.

Q. None of that was anything close to being legally true or even making sense.

A. Then why don't you write *I'm So Smart and I Know All About the Castle Doctrine*?

Q. Would you murder me if I did?

A. No; that book sounds stupid. Have at it.

8

Confidence

Do or do not: there is no try. —**Mahatma Gandhi**

I knew this guy, Bill, and he had a big problem he believed he just couldn't overcome. "There's no way I'm going to get out of this," he'd whine.

And I'd tell him, "Shut up, Bill. You're a whiny loser. And do you know why? You don't believe in yourself."

So I took Bill out to a nightclub and told him, "I want you to find the most attractive woman here and get her number."

"I don't know—"

I slapped him. "That's your inner hippie telling you to doubt yourself. And you're going to pop that hippie in the mouth by doing this anyway. You're Bill—a powerful man who can conquer himself—and this is a simple task for you. Do you believe that?"

"Yes, I do!" Bill said. And he walked over to a beautiful woman most other guys were too intimidated to approach. And because Bill believed in himself, the woman responded to Bill's inner power, and soon he came back with her number.

Now that Bill knew he could achieve anything he put his mind to, his initial problem—beating a murder charge in court—was easy to overcome.

Which was pretty bad, actually, because the guy was guilty as sin. Ends up he's a serial killer. I guess I really should look into the backgrounds of people before I help them; there are some crazy people out there.

Wait, did I track down that woman whose number he got and warn her? I think I did. . . .

Anyway, the point is that if you're going to succeed at awesome and believe that the hippie trying to drag you down from the inside can be beaten silent, you're going to need confidence. Doubt is just another name for that inner hippie trying to stop you from action. As we've said, hippies are lazy, and the hippie inside you knows he can continue to waste his life away if he can just break your confidence and keep you from acting out the awesomeness brewing inside you. So you have to shut up that hippie of doubt, and you will do that by fanning your confidence into a supernova that will melt the face off your inner hippie.

And this is why confidence is the cannon on your tank of awesome: It blows away the obstacles that keep you from being awesome. In a way, you need confidence to work on the other parts of being awesome—independence, gratitude, and ambition—because without confidence you might think you won't succeed at those or that it won't be worthwhile.

Hmm . . . Maybe I should have started with confidence in this book before I went on to talk about the other three.

No, what am I talking about? I know exactly what I'm doing. Confidence was the perfect part of the tank of awesome to end with.

Anyway, confidence is your cannon. Whatever stands in the way of your progress you will blow away with a depleted uranium shell of "Yes, I can!" Did you know that the modern tank shell contains no explosives? "Then how does it blow up enemy vehicles?" you're probably wondering. It does it with its pure awesomeness (and lots of kinetic energy).* And that's what you want your confidence to be: a projection of your inner awesomeness that can destroy anything in your way.

So the last thing you want is your inner hippie sticking flowers down that gun barrel. He will try to emasculate you,

---

* Source: Google.

to break your confidence, and you can't let him do this . . . unless you're a serial killer. Then, you know, definitely don't have confidence. In fact, please stop reading this book, as the knowledge contained within it will make you unstoppable, and we don't want that. Well, I don't want that.

BEING A VICTIM

As I've lectured you on how to be awesome, you may have thought of some people or things that are keeping you from being all you can be. I want you to list all those things. Go ahead and do it. This isn't a trick.

Did you do it? Then you're a whiny loser! This was a trick!

Focusing on external things holding you back is what your inner hippie wants, as he wants you to be a victim. He wants to lie about, going, "Woe is me! All the forces of the universe are against me! I can never achieve anything!" And then the one who is really victimizing you is yourself. There is no force out there that will hold you back as much as the hippie inside you.

So what do you do if there are things working against you, like racism, sexism, a disability, or me tricking you? It's the same as with punching your inner hippie: You be awesome. You strike back at everything working against you by being the best you can be and having confidence in yourself despite whatever obstacles you face. You say things like, "I don't care that you keep tricking me and calling me a loser in your book, Frank; I'm going to be so awesome that I'll write a book ten times better than yours."

No, wait; don't say things like that. You're not going to be able to write a better book than mine. That's stupid.

Anyway, you're never really a victim until you listen to your inner hippie about feeling sorry for yourself. Well, I guess you are a real victim if you're being murdered by a serial killer. And if the serial killer is Bill, mea culpa.

HAVE CONFIDENCE IN YOUR ABILITY

You may be thinking, "You talk about the importance of confidence, but don't hippies seem pretty confident at times?" Well, yes, they do, but only about preaching nonsense. In fact, it's hard to beat a hippie's confidence when it comes to talking about complete idiocy like how socialism will work or that SUVs are destroying the world or that hemp is super useful for absolutely everything. But this nonsense, of course, is just part of the hippie's aggressive uselessness. When people are trying to accomplish things, the hippie just wants to lounge around and act like he knows things, when actually the only thing a hippie is an expert at is getting punched in the face.

But anyone can be confident in the garbage they spout—someone could even write a whole book of stuff they just totally made up—but that doesn't help anyone. Instead, to get beyond your inner hippie, you need confidence in your ability. You need to be secure in what you're able to accomplish, and this confidence is anathema to your inner hippie.

Why? As I said before, your inner hippie wants you to think things are out of your hands—that you're a victim—so you don't even try to undertake new things because you believe they're beyond you. Then instead of doing anything useful, you'll sit around and spout hippie nonsense like, "We don't have to work; we can just tax the rich to pay for everything." Hey, if you try to take my money, I will come after you and punch your face. And the government won't be able to protect you, because I am unstoppable, since I have confidence in my ability to find people and punch them really hard to make them think twice about their nonsense.

And that's what you need: confidence that you can pull off whatever you set your mind to. Unlike with having confidence in nonsense you prattle on about, confidence in your ability leads to results. It's a confidence that keeps you moving forward, not lounging around, blathering about Karl Marx. Man, Karl Marx was such a stupid, long-haired hippie. If only someone had set him on the right path by punching him in the face, maybe he could have done something useful with his life—like maybe making duck calls like those guys from *Duck Dynasty*. He certainly had the beard for it.

Karl Marx pulling his blue plastic cup of iced tea out of his coat.

Anyway, don't be like Karl Marx and have confidence in your stupid communist theories; put that confidence into your ability to get achievable results. Be more like Marx's brother Groucho, who had confidence in his comedic ability.

CONFIDENCE NEAR INSANITY

In trying to break your confidence, you inner hippie will use a trick he's never used before: logic and reason. Usually, the lazy, stupid hippie inside you would run from basic logic and reason, but here he'll actually wield it in a bad-faith attempt to stop your awesome. "Just think rationally," he'll say. "You can't do all these grand plans of yours." He may even lay out a reasonable-sounding list of reasons you can't succeed at whatever you are currently attempting. "You can't make an army of dinosaurs with rocket launchers on them, because science can't yet genetically resurrect dinosaurs. And even if it could, there's no reason they'd follow your commands."

Whatever you do, don't listen. You need to just sucker-punch that hippie by loudly declaring, "Yes, I can!" and keep moving. Awesome does not slow down—your tank should just keep rolling forward no matter what—and thus there is no time for doubt.

But you may ask, "What if there are reasonable objections to what I'm trying to do?" Who cares? We're not talking about being reasonable; we're talking about being awesome.

In fact, confidence, when done right, should look like a form of insanity—but it's not insanity. When you're careening ahead in a rocket car of awesome, it's mind-boggling to behold and may scare and confuse others. Should you be worried about the reactions of others? Of course not, because you're confident, stupid! You know what you're doing. Who cares what a bunch of losers think? And dinosaurs with rocket launchers on them are the key to military dominance in the twenty-first century and are completely feasible. If any scientists say otherwise, then fire them and get new ones. If you're going to wear a white lab coat and then spend your entire day not making dinosaurs, your existence is completely pointless.

So as you march forward with confidence, if people yell, "You're insane!" that just means you're doing it right.

PRACTICING CONFIDENCE

Of course, your inner hippie is going to do everything he can to make you stop believing in yourself. You can best punch back by accomplishing awesome things, but maybe you'll need a little confidence boost before you can do that. Here are some ways to help build your confidence.

Talk to a mirror. Find a mirror, look yourself in the eye, and tell yourself how awesome you are. "I am a raging inferno of awesome. I am unstoppable. Countries—nay, worlds!—will bow before me. Anything I decide to do I can do better than anyone else." If you feel yourself starting to raise an objection to any of this, yell, "Shut up!" Note, you're not yelling shut up at yourself but at the hippie inside you trying to break you down. Maybe you should turn away from the mirror when yelling, "Shut up!" so as not to confuse yourself.

Talk to someone else. Of course, being confident in private is no real trick. So you need to do the mirror exercise, but this time while looking at someone else instead of a mirror. You can pick anyone—your boss, a girl you're trying to pick up at a bar, a police officer—and just tell him or her you're an unstoppable force of awesome. And if the person you're telling it to looks like he or she is going to object, yell, "Shut up!" Make a threatening motion if necessary.

Positive visualization. You can also improve your confidence by focusing on succeeding. When you have a task to do, first spend some time imagining yourself doing that task. And then imagine that ninjas attack. Now you're frantically working on the task while taking quick breaks to fend off ninja attackers—no, you're performing the task with one hand while blocking and striking against your enemies with the other, because that is how unbelievably awesome you are. As you defeat the last ninja, you also finish your task better than anyone has ever done it before. Everyone basks in your glory. The mayor hands you the key to the city. The deli next door names a sandwich after you.

Walk on hot coals. Walking on hot coals has often been used as a confidence booster, because, you know, they're really hot, and you normally wouldn't walk on them, so if you do you're like walking on stuff way hotter than you usually do, so—BOOM!—confidence. I don't know if they're supposed to be special coals or what, but . . . well, don't overthink this, or you're going to lose confidence. Just throw some hot coals down somewhere and walk on them.

Deep breathing. A simple confidence booster you can try anywhere, such as in the hospital getting your feet treated for third-degree burns, is to do some deep breathing. This is because relaxed people are confident people. If you know you will always succeed at everything, what do you ever have to worry about?

You might want to do some visualization while breathing. I like to imagine when I inhale that I'm pulling all the power of the earth into my body. And when I exhale, I'm casting my inner hippie out of my body. By the end of my breathing exercise, I feel like I'm bursting with power—like I could explode at any second and take out a city block. But that's just how I relax; you may relax differently, like by thinking of a beach or something.

Smile. Confident people smile. When you know you're the personification of awesome that can destroy problems like a sledgehammer can destroy Fabergé eggs, why wouldn't you smile? So one idea is to smile like you're confident to make yourself feel confident.

Now, there is a particular smile for that. You go too big on the smile, and the smile is more like, "I have this great plan to poison the water supply in Gotham City!" Instead, you want more of a slight, cocky smile—the kind Han Solo would have when spouting nonsense about parsecs to gullible farm boys. The kind of smile that says, "Yeah, I'm better than you, and I know it." If people start glaring at you like, "I want to wipe that stupid smile off his arrogant face!" then you've got it right.

FACE YOUR FEARS

So do you think you're confident now?

If you are confident, you will have responded to that question with "What do you mean, 'think'?! I *know* I'm confident. In fact, I don't even need this stupid book anymore; I can do everything myself!"

Did you answer that way? Good. And don't throw this book away. If you're this far into it, you might as well finish.

So now that you know you're confident, you need to test yourself by facing your greatest fear. Remember: You're confident, so you should fear nothing. And you need to prove it.

Let's say you have a phobia of spiders. Then you need to find a whole bunch of spiders and just grab a handful and eat them. Now spiders are scared of you, because you eat spiders! Though I don't know if spiders can be poisonous and you shouldn't eat them. Maybe you should look that up first.

Nah. Looking stuff up will just allow time for fear to grow. Quickly, go eat some spiders!

And if you're afraid of heights, then you need to go sky-diving.

Actually, no, that's a stupid idea, because you'll just become less and less scared the closer you get to the ground. Oh, go walk a tightrope. Do that one.

Of course, your inner hippie is going to scream at you when you face your fears. He doesn't want you to be this confident person who can take on anything, because then you have no excuses anymore. When you're facing your greatest fear, once again you're really taking on that hippie inside you who fills you with doubt. But you need to suplex him. Into a bunch of spiders' nests. Because he was the one who had the fear, not you. You're a tank of awesome, and tanks fear nothing. Except antitank aircraft.

Hmm. Maybe we need a fifth part of being awesome that can be a surface-to-air missile battery . . .

Nah. We're good.

SUMMARY OF CHAPTER 8: CONFIDENCE

In this chapter, we learned:

- There is a serial killer on the loose.
- Confidence is a cannon that can blow things up with the power of your delusions.
- Something about not being a victim.
- Don't have the type of confidence where you talk nonsense, but instead where you do nonsense and call it awesome, I guess.
- Basically be insane, but that's sort of been the theme of this whole book.
- There are a number of ways to practice confidence, but I'm kind of doubtful about all of them.
- Eat spiders, even though they may or may not be poisonous.

Since you've now finished building your tank of awesome, in the next chapter we'll focus on living a hippie-free life.

Study Questions

Remember a time you were really confident. How did you feel then? Why can't you feel that way all the time? Are you stupid or something?

Why do you think we develop phobias? Shouldn't we focus more on making other things develop phobias of us?

If you help someone and it turns out he's a serial killer, does that count as a good deed? I mean legally, like if you had a community service requirement to fill.

ANSWERS TO COMMON QUESTIONS

Q. Aren't there some things you shouldn't be confident about? For instance, if you're five feet tall, you're not going to win a dunking competition.
A. What are you talking about? You'll just have to jump higher to do it.

Q. But I mean there are just some things that are unrealistic—
A. I'll just stop you there. If you want my permission to fail at anything, I'm not going to give it. Shut up, hippie. There is no "impossible"; there are just things you're still in the process of figuring out. And you will. Because confidence.

Q. Can't the confidence you describe be dangerous, especially if it's confidence to do something that in fact could lead to grave harm?

A. That's just the inner hippie in your head trying to pretend to use logic to discourage you.

Q. Or maybe it's just the logic in my head logically discouraging me.

A. Well, you can't be sure, so just ignore anything your mind says.

Q. And I don't get the whole walk-on-hot-coals thing; why go out of your way to do something dangerous like that when there are plenty of non-hot places to walk?

A. Because it helps you build confidence! Also, it could be useful if maybe a volcano goes off near you and you need to escape, but the only path to escape is over hot coals, and you don't have shoes.

Q. That seems unlikely.

A. Your face seems unlikely.

Q. The way you came back with a petty insult perhaps shows you don't have confidence in your own opinions.

A. Hey, don't try to psychoanalyze me. Many have tried before, and I always got my money back in the end.

Q. Any update on Bill the serial killer?

A. Oh, I wouldn't worry about him. Serial killers always mess up and get caught . . . you know, after they kill enough times.

9

Living a Hippie-Free Life

Stay frosty.   —Sun Tzu

Michael was a successful guy. He was the CEO of a major corporation and had a large, beautiful house and probably a fulfilling family life, though I kind of zone out when people talk about that sort of thing. He had obviously conquered his inner hippie and was rolling happily along in his tank of awesome on the path of success.

But things started to change. He seemed increasingly disinterested in his work and was no longer as focused on the task at hand. It was like his tank had rolled into a ditch—and it's hard to push a tank out of a ditch, because it is heavy and big. Still, even in a ditch I guess you could still move the cannon around and blow stuff up, which is fun and cool—but now we're stretching the metaphor beyond what I intended.

Anyway, the point is Michael had previously conquered his inner hippie, but now he seemed to be failing again. So I asked him, "What's the matter? Are you on drugs?"

"No."

"You shouldn't be doing drugs."

"I'm not doing drugs."

"Well, since you're not using your drugs, can I have them?"

"I don't have any drugs."

"I'm not going to take them. I just want to see what they'd do to a squirrel."

"There aren't any drugs."

I nodded thoughtfully. "All right. Then what is the problem?"

Michael was silent for a moment. "I just wonder if what I'm doing is worth all this time and hard work. Is success really just advancing up the corporate ladder and acquiring more money and stuff? For instance, I keep hearing about wars and famine and climate change and other things that are devastating this planet. Shouldn't I be putting my efforts into important things like that—things way more important than corporate greed? Maybe I need to quit my job and really try to help people and spread the word about what society should be focusing on. What do you think?"

There were tears in my eyes as I gave him my response. "Shut up, hippie." And I punched him in the face.

It's very sad when someone who was awesome relapses into hippieness, but it can happen to anyone. You may have beaten your inner hippie into a broken mess just lying there on the floor and feel you're secure, but it may not always be that way. Sure, the first couple of times that he wakes up enough to utter anything, you walk over and kick him, but maybe later you get lazy about it and begin ignoring him, figuring he's beaten. And eventually you look over, and there is your inner hippie, sitting up and smoking a joint and saying, "You should just chill a bit, dude." And, thinking there is no harm in it now, you listen. And soon you're on a downward spiral as your inner hippie grows stronger and you grow weaker until one day a caring individual punches you in the face.

Yes, if you follow the advice of the previous chapters, you will conquer your inner hippie and build an unstoppable tank of awesome, but to keep that tank rolling, you must continually maintain it. And to keep your inner hippie quiet, you must continuously punch him. So we want to make sure you continue to live your hippie-free life so that you never relapse and give up your awesome to whine about global nonsense or something.

ACCOMPLISHMENTS JOURNAL

One way to make sure you keep up your awesome, hippie-free lifestyle is to keep track of the awesome you accomplish every day. I don't mean write in a diary—you're not a nine-year-old girl (but if you are a nine-year-old girl reading this book to learn to be more awesome, God bless you)—but instead just have some place where you write down what you did today. Don't write thoughts or feelings or other useless crap—I mean "useless junk." Now I have it in my head that a nine-year-old girl is reading this and I need to watch my language.

Anyway, in your journal, don't write down feelings but instead just your actual accomplishments of awesome. For instance, I'll write in mine today: "Wrote in my book a great idea about recording your accomplishments each day; drop-kicked a raccoon." And hopefully you'll remember through-out the day that you're going to be evaluating what you've done, so don't listen to that inner hippie when he tells you to loaf around; you punch that guy, and you get things done so you'll have something worth bragging about to write down at the end of the day.

THE BUDDY SYSTEM

It's tough to look at your own self objectively. I've known a number of people who thought they were doing great, and then I had to inform them that, no, their lives were awful, and they were making me sick. That's why the buddy system is a good way to make sure you don't backslide toward hippiedom. It's good to have a partner you can trust who will help watch for signs you're giving in to the hippie inside you instead of stomping on him, tell you when you're just not being awesome, and point out when you're whining. Basically, you need someone to criticize all your flaws as they become visible. I find that a spouse especially loves this job. In fact, this seems to be the job my wife was born to do, as she can loudly point out my flaws with an unrivaled zeal. She even recently asked if I could do the same for her, but I've been married long enough to know that that's a trick and have instead been telling her that everything she does is awesome.

Sometimes the buddy system can fail—like when Michael took out a restraining order against me—but overall it's a great way to make sure you stay on the path of awesome. Plus, I just really like criticizing others if anyone needs a buddy.

HANG WITH THE RIGHT PEOPLE

In trying not to relapse into your old hippie ways, you may need to stay out of the atmosphere you previously lived in. That means maybe ditching your old loser friends who don't share your feelings about being awesome. As for your new friends, make sure they are only the most awesome people around, without a trace of hippie inside them. If you have trouble finding friends like these, maybe instead build one by making a robot. Robots always make the coolest friends, and you can't not be awesome with a robot following you around. Just make sure you program it well so it shows no signs of being a hippie. You may have to modify the three laws of robotics for that. Usually, those are:

1. Don't harm people.
2. Follow orders.
3. Preserve self.

So you'll want to add a fourth law—Don't be a hippie—in there. I'm not sure if you should put it before or after the "don't harm people" law. Oh, and also add maybe a fifth law that says, "Don't strangle puppies," because I don't think any of the other laws cover that one, and no one will like your robot friend if he goes around strangling puppies.

STAY PHYSICALLY FIT

Being awesome can be strenuous. And if you don't have the energy for it, you'll be more likely to listen to your inner hippie when he tells you, "Hey, relax a bit. This can all wait for later." And then you sit for a minute and relax and close your eyes, and the next thing you know, you're participating in a protest about some national issue you can't coherently explain and burning an American flag. Because your inner hippie will use any weakness to grab hold of you, so you need the energy to resist his siren call of laziness. For that, you need to be physically fit.

Useful Exercise

Most people think that being physically fit means joining a gym and exercising. If you've ever exercised before, you've come to the realization that it is awful and pointless. "I'm going to lift heavy things for no reason and then jog around to get to no place in particular. Maybe I'll pedal a bike that doesn't go anywhere." It's so stupid and just feels like a huge waste of time. I mean, you may help yourself by doing this, but you'll still feel like a useless hippie. And you have to trust your gut, because at this point your gut should really hate hippies.

Now, did the frontiersmen of America's past do pointless exercises every day? No, instead they did useful activities that kept them physically fit. They chopped wood, plowed fields, and karate-chopped grizzly bears—all things that actually had to be done but that also made sure they got their exercise.

This is all well and good if you have a nice, healthy, physical job like coal mining, but in the modern world many of us have jobs where we just sit around in front of a computer all day. And those jobs pay well, too, as no one likes computers. They're awful; they're complicated, have bright screens that hurt your eyes, and sometimes like to spy on you for the government. And you can't get exercise while using them. Have you ever tried jogging while holding a laptop? You'll run right into a lamppost and smash your computer. I hope you backed up that Excel spreadsheet in the cloud.

By the way, does anyone know where the cloud is? It has a lot of my files.

Anyway, you'll need to try to find some useful activities to do on the side that will get you exercise. Here are some suggestions:

- Gardening
- Hunting
- Fight club
- Cattle rustling
- Invading another country

So find a physical hobby that sounds interesting to you and make sure you stay physically fit. Being awesome can be quite taxing, and I find I often have to run away from mobs of people really fast.

Eating Right

In addition to getting exercise, you also need to eat right to keep yourself full of energy and ready to be awesome. People make this way too complicated. You'll constantly see all this contradictory science, such as saying that a certain food causes cancer, and then the next day the same food cures cancer, and after that they'll say that same food wards off vampires, and then later it is actually vampires' favorite food. You'll eventually realize that, while a few scientists develop awesome tech like lasers and DVRs, the majority are apparently useless idiots who have no idea what they're talking about. Basically just hippies in white lab coats. If some scientist comes to you and starts telling you what you should or shouldn't eat, punch him in the face[*] and yell, "Did your computer model tell you that was going to happen?"

And if he says, "Yes, it did," and shows you a printout as proof, then he might be one of the good scientists, and you should apologize.

---

[*] Because he's a hippie.

Anyway, people have lots of different ideas of what you should eat these days, and hippies are especially vocal about it. They're all, "You have to eat organic, free-range quinoa that's free of hormones and genetic modification." And, of course, your instinct is to punch them and jam a fistful of bacon into your mouth—and I can't say that instinct is wrong. Because your body knows what it wants to eat, and it signals this to you by making some things taste good and other things taste awful. Some people think you have to work against that, but that's stupid. Humanity was around long before healthy eating crazes, and people just ate what they could find. And okay, maybe they didn't live that long back then, but they lived long enough to get things done and eventually lead to the society we have today.

So let's not complicate eating. You need to eat what tastes yummy, and then just take a look at your weight. If you weigh too much, then eat less than what you've been eating. If you're underweight, eat a bit more than what you've been eating. If you weigh just right, then keep eating that same amount; don't deviate from it.

You're probably now asking, "Well, should I eat junk food and high-fructose corn syrup?" To which I say, I don't know. I'm not a scientist. And if I were a scientist, I still wouldn't know, and you probably shouldn't listen to me. My only advice to you is if you eat something you think might be bad for you, just make sure it's really yummy. If it's going to shorten your life, at least then you'll get yumminess out of it. What you don't want to do is eat stuff that's bad for you that you don't find tasty; now that would just be pointless.

But I don't like this idea of eating nonyummy stuff that's supposed to be healthy and keep you alive a long time. Who wants to live forever eating only bland, tasteless stuff like vegetables? That sounds like a horrible life I wouldn't wish on my worst enemy (well, come to think of it, I might wish that on Carl; I hate Carl so much!). And eating right is no guarantee that you'll live a long time. You could have a nice salad and then walk outside and get hit by a bus. And then what will your last thought be? "I should have just gone ahead and had that bacon cheeseburger." You don't want to live a life of regret, so eat tasty things.

RAISING KIDS

One day, a woman came to me in tears (what is it with women and crying?). "I'm afraid my children are hippies!" she said. "They all act so entitled and never do their chores or any work!"

And I told her, "All kids are like that."

Her tears dried up some. "So there's nothing to worry about?"

I shook my head. "No. I didn't say that. What I meant to

say was all kids are like that . . . and that's awful and must be crushed."

As you've probably noticed, children are a lot like the worst hippies. They do no useful work, and they expect everything to just be handed to them. But it's not as bad as with an adult hippie, because it's not like they've rejected hard work and responsibility—they just don't know about it yet. It's like each child's inner hippie is this super-annoying and loud one—but he's also standing right next to a cliff. So with the proper shove, the hippie will plummet to his doom, breaking his bones against the jagged rocks below. And it's your job as a parent to help your child give the hippie that push and laugh at his violent impact.

If you listen to any little kid—and you should listen to your own kids from time to time, despite the fact that most of what they say is nonsense—you'll hear lots of big plans of becoming an astronaut or a fireman or the daughter of royalty. That's because within each child is the innate desire to be awesome. Your job is to make them understand that the only way to be awesome is through responsibility and hard work. "Little Billy, if you don't work hard, all your dreams will fail, and you will die sad and alone." Your children may then ask if you'll still love them if that happens. I think you're legally required to answer yes to that, but don't really sell it. Let them always question that one.

So as soon as their little arms are big enough to lift things, you get them to work. "Fun must be earned"—that will be their new motto. You should probably also come up with a saying for potty training, as you don't want them to pee on your stuff.

Your goal will be that by the time your children are teenagers, they will have learned so much responsibility that they will entirely skip adolescence. Adolescence, from the Latin word *adolescere*, which means—well, we don't really have an English equivalent, but it's basically a word for the desire to grab something by the neck and shake it—is a sort of hyperconcentrated hippiedom that modern kids experience when they begin having near-adultlike abilities but have no responsibilities. This leaves them all day to think useless thoughts while listening to horrible music that sounds like someone beat a cat to death with a synthesizer and wearing hideous clothes that look like they were picked out by a color-blind court jester. And the worst thing about this hippie-ism is that you can't even legally punch teenagers until they're eighteen.[*]

There didn't used to be adolescence in the olden days. When you hit thirteen, you got married and were sent off to war or the coal mines. Teenagers had no time to be annoying and useless, because if you didn't mine enough coal each day, you were put in the stocks. But nowadays we coddle

---

[*] Again, I'm just assuming that's how the laws on punching work. Check with your lawyer.

teenagers and support their uselessness, and even Amazon doesn't sell stocks anymore (I searched for "stocks" there and just got a bunch of books on Wall Street). And with our push to send all kids to college now, we've actually extended adolescence, making it even longer until our children's inner hippies first meet the vicious punch of the real world.

You don't want this for your children. When they are old enough, you let them know that while your love is free and infinite, everything else costs money and is finite. You will cut them off as soon as you legally can, and then they have to earn their own keep. The teenagers will probably protest this—as they protest every sensible thing—saying things like, "Hey, daddio, but all my friends' parents buy them lots of things, and they don't have to get jobs. Why do you have to be a square?"*

You then tell them, "All your friends are useless idiots who will die in the next natural disaster—which I hope comes soon, since I hate them. But you will learn to be a responsible, useful citizen, or you are no child of mine. And I don't mean that as an idle threat; I'll get a DNA test and fake the results so that legally you're no longer my child." Tough love.

---

*   I don't know what slang kids use today, and I don't want to know.

SURVIVING A COLLEGE CAMPUS

An especially challenging situation in which to punch your inner hippie and make sure he stays down is when you are a student on a college campus. There you will be surrounded by hippie influences telling you you don't have to work hard, that you should just let your parents pay for everything, and that all your idiot ideas denouncing the hard work of others are great. And you can't even punch the hippies; colleges often have strict rules about not punching professors or the staff.

And the professors are the worst. Yes, we all know about obnoxious college students with a drop of knowledge but not even a jot of experience who think they've got economics and politics and morality all figured out, but one day they'll graduate, and then the real world is just going to pound the crap out of them. I mean really brutalize those idiots until their faces are wet with their own tears about the harshness of the real world. It will be hilarious.

But some keep their hippie selves safe from the real world. They stay on the college campus and become professors—spouting absolute nonsense about how the world is without ever actually venturing into it and getting those ideas dashed to pieces on the jagged rocks of reality. And if those people receive the treasured blessing called tenure, then they become hippies forever. And that's what college basically is: a Neverland for hippies, where hippies can live free from reality and never grow up.

So if you're a college student, you will need to live in this Neverland while never letting yourself become a part of it. Consider yourself as someone who knows he is trapped in the Matrix. You'll try to blend in so as not to arouse suspicion, but you know in your heart that none of this is real and that the real world lies outside it. So smile, get along, get your good grades, and then get that diploma, which is your key to breaking out of the Matrix and into reality. And while the others will scream and cry at the harshness of the real world, you'll celebrate finally being free.

Well . . . unless you go on to graduate school. Then you'll have to resist the system again, and there are limits. Few people make it to a PhD without getting pulled in by the hippie-call of college. If you immerse yourself in it too much, you will be assimilated. I might be mixing sci-fi metaphors.

CONTUNDE DIEM

One of the problems with punching your inner hippie is that it can get boring after a while. When you've fully conquered him, it's little challenge to just kick him every so often when he makes a sound. And while this is necessary, it will no longer satisfy your desire to pummel something. You see, according to science,* man is born with an innate desire to punch things. For a while, you will satisfy that urge by punching your inner hippie, but as it takes less punching to get him to shut up, you'll need to find something else to curb-stomp. Here's what I suggest you then beat up: the day.

I have a motto I live by: *Contunde diem.* It's Latin for "Pwn the day."† You see, each day is a special gift—a gift you should focus on pounding until it gives you everything it has. To truly pwn the day, you must take each day, tie it to a chair, and start beating it with a rubber hose while yelling, "Give me everything you have! I demand it all!"

And the day will plead with you. "I gave you so much! Can't you just relax a little and wait for the next day?"

And that's when you get the car battery.

"What are you going to do with that?" the day will scream.

You'll touch the clamps of the jumper cables together, creating sparks. "I know you have more to give me. And I will get it."

You can't have mercy for the day. You must send it away limping and bloody with tears in its eyes, so thankful that midnight has finally come. And then the next day will see

---

* By "science," I mean that it seems really true to me.

† Prove it isn't.

you with fear in its eyes and will try to run, but the day cannot escape you.

So after beating up your hippie, beat up the day. Make each day give you all it has. That's one of the secrets to being awesome: day torture.

SUMMARY OF CHAPTER 9: LIVING A HIPPIE-FREE LIFE

In this chapter, we learned:

- Frank needs drugs.
- You need to write in a diary, find someone who will yell at you, and maybe build a robot.
- You need to find productive things to do that also give you exercise, and you need to eat right . . . maybe. I didn't really get his conclusion there.
- Kids are hippies you can't legally punch (though I don't really think you can legally punch anyone).
- For some reason, you hate the day and want to hurt it.

In the next chapter, we'll talk about how to hippie-punch society.

Study Questions

Is there ever a reason to stop punching your inner hippie? If you answered "no," why didn't you answer "double no"? Are you secretly sympathizing with hippies?

Do you think your children will eventually learn to appreciate and respect you for the tough love you showed them when they were young? And if not, will it be good enough if they just know better than to try to mooch off of you when they're older?

How does it feel when you believe you've gotten the most out of the day? Does it feel like you made the day scream for mercy? If not, why did you go easy on the day? Are you secretly sympathizing with the day?

ANSWERS TO COMMON QUESTIONS

Q. If, no matter how much you punch your inner hippie, it's always waiting to take over in a moment of weakness, does that mean your inner hippie is essentially unkillable?

A. Just like evil will never be truly defeated and requires eternal vigilance, the same goes for laziness and whininess. Think of your inner hippie as Jason from *Friday the 13th*; no matter how many times he's supposedly killed, he always comes back for a sequel. Or maybe they did stop making those movies, so I guess the only thing that could really kill your inner hippie is dwindling box-office returns.

Q. How does that help me?
A. I already forgot the question. *Freddy vs. Jason* was pretty cool.

Q. Did your punching Michael help turn things around for him?
A. No. He called the cops on me, and then I had to spend the rest of the day explaining to the police that Michael had become a stupid hippie and that I was a licensed therapist applying a special technique to help him.

Q. Did that convince the police?
A. No. They asked to actually see my therapy license, and things sort of broke down from there.

Q. What's "pwn" mean?
A. Oh man, you're such a n00b.

Q. First, you told us to personify all the things in our lives that hold us back as this hippie inside of us, and

then you urged us to beat and injure it. Now you also talk about personifying the day and torturing it. Is this personifying things to inflict violence on them psychologically healthy?

A. Sure. It's healthy to imagine inflicting violence on things you hate.

Q. Are you a sociopath?

A. I dunno . . . but then again, I don't care if I am.

10

Hippie-Punching Society

Give a man a fish, shut him up for a day. Punch a man hard enough in the face, keep him from whining about his lack of fish for life.

—Plato

Every so often, I'll hear this from someone who followed all my advice: "I have a problem."

To which I say, "How could you? Didn't you do everything I said?"

And he'll say, "Yes, I followed *all* your advice. I am now the embodiment of all that man can achieve. Nations bow before me. Mountains shudder in my presence. Squirrels scamper away if I get too close. But I still have a problem."

"And what's that?"

"Other people."

Yes, once you follow all my advice, you'll start to encounter the same problem I've had since an early age: complete disgust at the living failures who are all the people around you. Sure, you've met your full potential as an American, but there are still these useless blobs of goo called your fellow men standing around in your way or just offending your sight.

So what do you do? As you've probably learned, each man can only punch his own inner hippie—he can only ever punch the outer hippie of another but can never really strike the true hippie essence that needs a beating. So do we just put up with everyone else? That's not an option, because I hate them too much; it pains me that they are around me, and I have a busy schedule and can't spend all day punching hippies and dealing with the hassles that come with that, such as the legal problems. (I keep explaining to the juries that they're hippies. How hard is that to understand?) So what we must do is take measures to try to improve this country as a whole, or as I call it, hippie-punching society.

STATUS QUO

Punching society is an appealing concept to lots of people. We often hear that society is to blame for so many things—

crime, illiteracy, fat kids—and if society had a face, I'm sure people would punch it all the time. But society has no face, and thus it always seems to escape the proper punishment it's due. Well, just like we had to get creative to punch our inner hippies, we'll also need to use special measures to give society the smackdown it deserves. And the way to punch society is to take on the status quo.

Everyone acts like they don't like the status quo. You usually only hear the term used negatively. "We need to change the status quo in Washington!" But the reason things never change meaningfully is that most people actually cling to the status quo. When a natural disaster like a hurricane hits a city and knocks out the power, you never hear people say, "Well, that sure shook up the status quo." Because people love the status quo; they like everything in society to be predictable and expected, and they like to believe that all the important things are being handled. They don't even really care if things are handled well as long as someone else is taking care of them. And it's that collective attitude that got us this giant, bloated government that only ever gets larger and fatter. The government is now like one of those eight-hundred-pound people who are confined to a bed. Yet everyone is convinced that if we just feed it more chicken wings, education will improve, everyone will have good health care, and we'll each receive a free pony.

Scientists estimate that at our current rate of government

spending, in fifty years the entire earth will be rendered un-inhabitable by debt, causing humanity to abandon the earth and try to set up a colony on Mars. Then the earth will be left in the hands of the monkeys we left behind (as they have no debt), and they'll probably blow up the Statue of Liberty.* So is that the future we want? One where, when people ask, "How's it look outside?" your answer will always be, "Pretty red"? We can individually be as awesome as we want, but eventually we'll have little room to do it as big, fatty government takes up all the space, surrounded by use-less blobs all going, "Hey, government, help us with stuff!" Those people will most likely die out in the first Martian war when we fight the natives of Mars who have remained hidden all this time.

So we need to hippie-punch society. We need people to see the potential they have if they break their habits of government reliance and dependency. In the least, I need people taking less of my money for their big, stupid gov-ernment that I hate. I like my money. It and I would do beautiful things together. But instead you're taking it for the government and then spending it stupid. It breaks my heart.

---

* Maybe this wasn't a scientific estimate; maybe it was just a weird dream I had.

SHAKING UP THE STATUS QUO

So it's pretty obvious that society needs us to shake up the status quo. We really need to grab the status quo, slap it around a bit, shove it into a metal garbage can, and then put the lid on the can and just keep banging the can with a stick until the status quo eventually emerges, disoriented and partially deaf. Now, how do we accomplish this? Anytime there's talk about cutting government and making people more self-reliant, people get all scared. "Without government programs, won't people starve and die?" You'll try to explain to them that we didn't always have all these entitlements bloating the government, and people did just fine. And then they'll ask, "But didn't some people starve and stuff back then?" And you'll say, "No one anyone really liked." But they never consider that a satisfying answer.

Still, here are some ways to challenge that status quo and give society the hippie-punching it needs to reform itself.

A Proper President

Everyone looks up to the president of the United States like he's the leader of our country. I don't get that. It's my understanding that he is in fact just the guy in charge of the

country's government, that is, he's the head of the least part
of this nation, the part that just gets in everyone's way while
the rest of us do all the actual work and innovation. So he's
basically the head idiot.

Still, people look to this guy to set the tone for the country, so one way to really shake things up for people would be
to finally elect a proper president. What would be a proper
president? Well, to demonstrate, here is what the inaugural
address of a good president would be:

*I have heard your complaints, people. The economy is
horrible. Health care is expensive. Schools are failing our
children. Unemployment is up. Monkeys have escaped
from the zoo. And I have thought long and hard on these
problems and have one thing to say:*

Shut.

Up.

*Really. I am sick and tired of hearing about your non-
problems like it's my job to do anything about them.
What are you? Invalids? Take care of your own little
problems and leave me alone.*

*Do you even understand who I am? I'm the leader
of the government. You know the government, right? A
place full of bureaucrats and other vindictive, incompetent idiots. And you want me to use these people to fix
what's wrong in your lives? That's like tasking a bunch*

of toddlers hyped up on sugar to fix your car, you bone-heads. Tell me what you want destroyed, and I'll point them at that, because that's about all you can count on them to do: destroy things.

You want to know what's wrong with this country? It's your whining. Because when you whine about your tiny little problems, then the politicians think they need to do something about them, and when this collection of nitwits we call the government tries to help, they just make things worse while costing us like a trillion bucks. And eventually we turn that little stuff you whine about into actual problems.

Well, no more. If you come to me and whine about your problems, I will punch you in the face. And then I will shove you into a crate and mail it to some third-world country so you can find out what actual problems are like. And I won't be doing this in my capacity as president; I will be doing it as a concerned citizen who hates how hippies are ruining everything and who is stronger than you and can shove you into a crate. So whatever you think is wrong, figure it out yourself. Can't afford gas. Can't find a job. You're starving. These are all things I don't care about, and I will hurt you for acting like I'm supposed to do something about them.

This is the last you will see of me for my term. I'm going to go to the White House basement and smoke a

*cigar while watching old war movies. If you come and
bother me for anything other than that another country
is invading us, then may God have mercy on your souls.*

Now, that would be a proper American president, one
who makes it clear we are not supposed to rely on him, so
people will finally learn to solve their own problems. Of
course, it will be hard to get someone like that in office,
since the people who run for office tend to be meddlesome
nitwits. They all have these big ideas to help the country but
only make big, expensive messes, since the best way for a
politician to help the country is to do nothing.

Anyway, I'll take the job of president if offered. I mean, it
pays like $400,000 a year and includes room and board, and
I won't actually do much but play video games all day while
everyone else handles their own crap. That's pretty decent.
Maybe then I could find some time to work on my rocket
boots project. You see, I want to make rocket boots like Iron
Man. We have the technology to make rockets and to make
boots, so it seems like someone should be able to put them
together. Anyone know where I can rent some orangutans
to test them on?

Anti-Whining Campaign

What's the biggest problem facing our nation? Childhood obesity, you say? Well, I hate fat kids as much as the next person, but whining is still a much bigger problem than even that.

As I've already discussed at length, whining is one of the worst things ever, and an essential part of being a hippie. If we are to hippie-punch society and obliterate the status quo, we need to strike out against whining in this country. In an ideal world, being accused of being a whiner would be worse than being accused of being a pedophile or a racist. Everywhere a whiner would go, people would shun him. And the whiner would probably say, "Stop being so mean to me!" . . . except he'd say it in a high-pitched, annoying voice. Whiners are the worst.

So maybe instead of all these ads trying to keep people from smoking cigarettes and doing meth, we should have some ads focused on telling people about the horrors of whining. Something like: "This is Edgar. At an early age, he got into whining and never stopped. Now he's overweight, unemployed, and hated by everyone. Don't let whining ruin your life, too. Whining: It makes you worse than Hitler."

And we need to train kids from a young age that whining is terrible. Like half of children's programming should be on the dangers of whining. And if you've ever been around little children, it's actually pretty odd that that isn't already the standard.

Can we stamp out whining in our time? Maybe, if we work hard at it. But if we can't, and whining still abounds, let's not complain too much about it. Because irony.

Bring Back Starving to Death

Do you know how many people starved to death in the United States of America last year? None. It's almost impossible to do here. You really have to go out of your way to make it happen, like by getting trapped down a well for a month with no one knowing that you're there. There are food stamps and dollar menus and ramen noodles—if you want food, it's out there and easily available.

But throughout history, not starving to death has been an essential motivator of mankind. Like we came up with farming to avoid dying from hunger. Farming is not natural for man; we normally hate plants and find it funny when they wither and die. But with the threat of starving to death to inspire us, we've developed advanced farming techniques, and now you can get avocados at basically any grocery store. Can you imagine life before guacamole? It was short and brutal.

But now with the incentive of not starving to death gone, we've all gotten lazy. Man used to have to stalk and hunt a deer for hours for his dinner, and now we can just lie back in a recliner and have pizza delivered. And if that takes more than thirty minutes, we demand it for free (even though that particular policy ended decades ago).

So a great way to hippie-punch society and really shake things up would be to bring back the threat of starving to death. And I don't mean it needs to be common, just that the possibility needs to be out there somewhere. We as a society need to just clearly define a certain point past which we will cease to give an able-bodied person free food. If you're obviously capable of work and for some reason aren't, there will be a point where no matter how much you beg or cry, we'll just stand back and let you starve. Again, it probably won't happen often, but think of what it will do for society if in the back of everyone's minds they know they can starve to death if they become lazy hippies. It will be just a little extra motivation inside everyone to push them forward to work and achieve and innovate. Nothing spurs creativity like the threat of dying horribly.

HIPPIE-PUNCHING OTHER COUNTRIES

Have you seen the other countries out there? They're all like dictatorships or quasi-dictatorships or European. It's awful. And even when America falters, none of them come even close to rivaling us. Luxembourg isn't going to police the world. Chile isn't going to lead in technological innovation. Uganda isn't going to make the next hit fast-food chain. People get worried about China because it's so big, but all they do is make our cheap plastic trinkets. I mean, that country is still run by the Communist Party. Did they not get the memo on what a dead end communism is? Do they also listen to eight-tracks over there? Come on.

You might be saying, "That's great. I like that America is so much better than all other countries. And I like laughing at the misfortunes of foreigners." And this is true, but part of what puts our country into a slump is not having a rival to spur us on to be better. There used to be countries nearly as good as we were that we had to best. And there used to be other countries out there with a realistic claim to being able to destroy us. Thus we worked hard here to compete with the other powerful countries and made ourselves stronger so we could fight off the countries that wanted to annihilate us. Like look at all the nukes we have. Do you think we would have built that many without something out there motivating us? I mean, sure, mushroom clouds are cool, but after seeing a dozen or so of them, they kind of get predictable and boring. So we probably would have only made a few nukes if it weren't for some other nation like the Soviet Union that we had to show up. If it weren't for them, we'd have barely any nukes lying around, and people wouldn't take us seriously.

I'm not saying we need a new enemy like the Nazis or the commies, but it would be nice to at least have a decent rival. It's like we're the NFL, and everyone else is a high school team; we don't even need to train hard to win. I mean, what do we have to do to be better than Canada? Exist. That's it.

So to benefit ourselves, we need to try to improve the other countries out there and get them to not suck so much; in other words, we need to hippie-punch other countries. Here are some ideas on how to do that:

Bombing

Probably the closest thing to hippie-punching a country is bombing it. Now, we don't bomb our own allies (even though that really might help encourage them to do better), but there are plenty of awful countries out there filled with tyrants, terrorists, and soccer teams that could only be improved by a good bombing. The mistake we often make in bombing other countries is that we then go in to help them rebuild after the devastation, but helping them out like that will only reinforce their hippielike ways. The idea here is to help these countries improve themselves, and part of that is letting them figure out how to rebuild their bombed-out countries on their own.

The objection I often hear to this is "Won't that make us

a hegemon?" But I don't know what that word means, and it sounds made up. The other objection I get is "What if when they rebuild their country they hate us and still want to do evil to us?" Well that's simple: Then we just bomb them again. We have lots of bombs; we can keep doing this over and over and over until the country finally figures out what it's doing wrong and fixes it. "Oh, that is why we keep getting bombed; if we just get rid of our dictatorship and stop hoarding chemical weapons, we'll be a much nicer country. Thanks for helping us figure that out, America!" If you don't think that will work, just remember all the countries the United States went to war with that we're now friends with: Britain. Germany. Japan. Half of Korea. Bombing just shows we care enough about a country's future to intervene.

Taxes and Fines

It's well known that the United States is the world's police force. Basically, our country is the cop mustache of the planet. But aren't police supposed to be supported by tax money from the community they police? So where are the contributions from the rest of the world to support America's policing? Sounds to me like a bunch of lazy hippies just mooching off us and the security we provide to the world. Well, no more. It's time we institute a property tax for living on Earth, since that is the place we police. Every foreign country out there is more work for us—we have to keep an eye on them and make embassies and whatnot—so it's time those countries foot the bill for that. Normally I'm against new taxes, but this one only affects foreigners, so it's not as objectionable.

. And what about the costs we incur when we have to go to bomb a country? That's for their betterment, yet we're always the one paying for everything. Thus we need a "we had to bomb you" fine. Man, I would not want to be a country that gets nuked by us; nukes are really expensive.

Better Olympics

So competition will help other countries improve, but the only real competition we commonly have between all nations is the Olympics. And the events we compete in there are utter nonsense. Running, swimming, luging—who cares about all that? No one ever said, "That country has a couple of people who can throw a disc really far; I bet they'll be the next superpower."

Instead, we need to change the Olympics to be a contest of things that actually matter for a country. Like there should be an event where countries create businesses and technology. And maybe a paintball tournament to see who's better at military maneuvers. Perhaps some sort of freedom competition where each government watches its citizens go about doing whatever they want to do, and the winner is whichever government can keep itself from interfering for the longest.

SUMMARY OF CHAPTER 10: HIPPIE-PUNCHING SOCIETY

In this chapter, we learned:

- If it wasn't obvious already, Frank hates people.
- Something about a quo's status and shaking it.
- A good president would just insult everybody and do nothing (haven't we already had that president?).
- Starving people need to stop whining.
- We should bomb and tax other countries and then see if they'll play paintball with us.

In the next chapter . . . oh, I think we're about done.

Study Questions

As a concerned citizen, is it your duty to hippie-punch society? Or is it simply something to do because everyone else annoys you so much?

Is it the responsibility of the government and the president to do anything other than crush countries that annoy us? If you think the government's role is more expansive than that, how long have you been a communist?

Why do we even have other countries than the United States?

ANSWERS TO COMMON QUESTIONS

Q. You say the perfect president would just yell at us and then not be seen for the rest of his term, but isn't it also the job of the president to inspire the nation?

A. I don't know where people got that idea. If you want to be inspired, hire a motivational speaker. I'm available, by the way. I get very good reviews . . . except by people who can't take my awesome intensity. Which are most. You know, a lot of people can't be motivated because they are awful people, and that's not really my fault. And I warned everybody that the first two rows might be exposed to open flames.

Q. Aren't there other things we should teach our kids than not to whine?

A. You've obviously never had kids.

Q. **We won't actually let anyone starve to death, right?**
A. The question is whether a perfectly capable individual will let himself starve to death. If some lazy punk wants to play chicken, I'll play chicken.

Q. **What if your idea to hippie-punch other countries just angers them?**
A. Then they'll yell at us, call us names, and make impotent vows to do something about us, that is, it will be a day that ends in *y*.

Q. **Instead of antagonizing other countries, shouldn't you try to learn what you can of their culture and values so you can enrich yourself?**
A. How did you make it this far in this book?

11

Final Thoughts

This has been a journey—probably the greatest journey you've ever embarked on.

—Frank J. Fleming

This has been a journey—probably the greatest journey you've ever embarked on. In the beginning, you were ruled by your inner hippie. You were a disgusting, lazy failure. Your existence shamed this country and all those who sacrificed to make it what it is. To even think of what you were before you read this book nauseates me. I can't even contemplate how you managed to live with yourself. But now look at you. You're okay now.

And what of your inner hippie? He lies still and beaten as you stand there, fist clenched, waiting for him to dare to move again. You conquered the worst inside yourself, and now you are the best you can be. You went into a cocoon a caterpillar and have now emerged a velociraptor in a jetpack wielding a chain saw. You are unstoppable. Fearsome. Awe-inspiring.

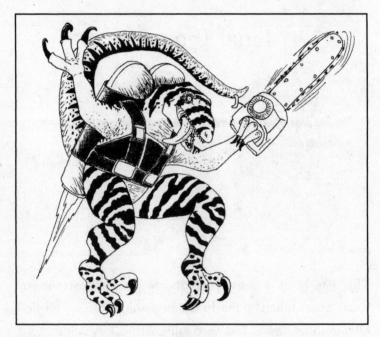

You.

So what's left? Just for you to go out and achieve great things. Yes, as soon as you finish reading this, you'll just start conquering the world. It is your destiny. And thus I'll keep this short, as you're probably saying, "Hey, wrap this up; I've got great things to achieve."

So I just want to remind you of one thing: You really owe me for getting you here. I mean, really, really owe me. For everything great you achieve, you should think in the back of your mind, "This only happened because of Frank." In fact, you should probably name a kid after me. Either have a new kid and name him after me or just rename one you already have. If it's a girl, you can call her Francine.

So did I have anything left? Let's see . . . I told you to achieve great things and to name a kid after me . . . I think that's it. I mean, you now know all about the root of failure—the hippie inside you—and you know the parts to building your tank of awesome—independence, gratitude, ambition, and confidence—and how to maintain your awesome and keep your hippie broken and beaten. You're now the pinnacle of mankind. You're prepared for anything. You could not be any better. You are an American.

So make each day count—in fact, make each moment count. You're free from the hippie inside you, and all barriers will fall to your tank of awesome. There is now no limit to what you can achieve. What a normal man would be thrilled to accomplish is utter, worthless garbage to you. Because you are that beyond-the-normal man now. You are practically a different species. *Homo hippiepunchicus.*

So remember: You will constantly face obstacles out there, things trying to slow you down or stop you. The government and regulations. Taxes. Meteors. Clamshell packaging. And it is your job to overcome everything out there. Because nothing really has the ability to stop you except the hippie inside you, and it has always been your choice whether to listen to him or punch him in his stupid hippie face. You can be as awesome as you choose to be. So go out there and accomplish something. If there's something out there you can't achieve, it's because you chose to fail. It's no one else's fault. And certainly not the fault of this book.

No refunds.

SUMMARY OF CHAPTER 11: FINAL THOUGHTS

In this chapter, we learned:

- That's the end of the book.
- I'm not really sure it needs a summary.
- Anyone still here?
- If you're in the publishing industry, can I send you a résumé?

And that's it! Good job being literate and finishing a book.

Study Questions

What does it feel like to have achieved perfection as a human being? Does it feel like having repeatedly punched someone whiny inside you? Because it should if you did it right.

How much will the author of this book be responsible for all you achieve after this? Should you send him a cut of all the millions you earn using his advice? If you answered no, why are you so greedy?

If you rated this book from one to five stars, what would you give it? If you said "five stars," would you be willing to write that on an online book site?

ANSWERS TO COMMON QUESTIONS

Q. So what's a hippie again?
A. Come on. You've read the whole book now; there shouldn't be any questions left.

Q. Actually, I have a few more questions on—
A. No, you don't. We're done. And frankly I'm getting tired of you and your stupid questions.

Q. Well, it's actually you writing the questions, so who are you really getting angry at?
A. Don't play your hippie mind tricks on me!

Q. You might have serious mental problems.
A. I might have serious awesome problems.

Q. I'm serious. This publicly arguing with yourself isn't normal.
A. "Blah blah blah." That's what you sound like.

Q. Fine. I'm leaving. I'm your last rational thought, and I'm going away.
A. Good. You've done nothing but hold me back.

Q. I'm serious. When I'm gone, you'll be left gibbering to yourself in a dark room.
A. Gibbering to myself in a dark room is how I do my best thinking.

Q. Fine. Them I'm out. I'm sick of you and your nonsense.
A. And you've done nothing but hold me back. With you finally gone, it will be nothing but punching hippies all day long.

Q. Have you ever even actually punched anyone?
A. . . .

A. Q-and-A is over.

About the Author

Frank J. Fleming is the author of *Obama: The Greatest President in the History of Everything* and *How to Fix Everything in America Forever*. He writes columns for PJ Media and the *New York Post*, and blogs at IMAO.us. Frank is a Carnegie Mellon University graduate and also works as an electrical and software engineer when he's not writing. He lives in Idaho with his wife and two kids. Frank is the country's leading advocate for nuking the moon.